the

HARROW
—FAIR—

cookbook

the
HARROW
FAIR
cookbook

MOIRA SANDERS

and

LORI ELSTONE

with

BETH GOSLIN MALONEY

FOREWORD *by*

ANNA OLSON

Prize-Winning Recipes
Inspired by Canada's Favourite
Country Fair

whitecap

Whitecap Books is known for its expertise in the cookbook
market and has produced some of the most innovative and
familiar titles found in kitchens across North America. Visit
our website at www.whitecap.ca.

Edited by Carolyn Stewart
Designed by Setareh Ashrafologhalai

Recipe photography by Mike McColl/General Chefery, including photos on page ix (bottom), 59, 62, 74, 118, 164, 208, 228
(top left, middle right, & bottom left), 236 (top right & middle
right), 237 (middle), and 238 (top right & middle left); food
styling by Moira Sanders and Lori Elstone.

Other photograph credits:
Moira Sanders: page ii (middle left & bottom left), viii (top
right), xii (bottom), xiv (bottom left), xvi (middle left &
middle right), 10, 25, 29, 42, 47, 51, 71, 78, 85, 86, 89, 150, 187,
224 (top left & bottom left), 226 (top left), 236 (top left), 237
(top), 238 (middle right)

Lori Elstone: page ii (top right), vi, xiv (top right), xvi (top
left), 34, 63, 81, 90, 140, 184, 224 (middle left), 227 (top,
middle, & bottom), 238 (top left & bottom left)

Beth Goslin Maloney: page viii (top left, middle left, & bottom
right), 16, 79, 190, 213, 224 (top right & bottom right), 226
(middle right), 228 (middle left), 236 (bottom left), 237 (bottom), 238 (bottom right)

Jake Elstone: page ii (top left, middle right, & bottom right),
viii (middle right & bottom left), ix (middle), xiv (top left,
middle right, & bottom right), xvi (top right, bottom left, &
bottom right), xviii, 3, 12, 14, 55, 56, 94, 117, 123, 142, 146, 159,
221, 224 (middle right), 226 (bottom left), 228 (top right &
bottom right)

Alan Sanders: page xii (middle), 18, 101, 132, 226 (top right &
middle left)

Matt Maloney: page 236 (bottom right)

Newspaper clipping on page xii (top) courtesy of *Harrow News*.
Photos on pages xiii, xiv (middle left), 154 (pictured: Mrs.
Belle Martin and Mrs. Mary Gorick), 226 (bottom right), and
236 (middle left) courtesy of Colchester South and Harrow
Agricultural Society. Photo on page 8 courtesy of the Essex
Region Conservation Authority.

Article from the *Windsor Star* on page 159 reprinted with
permission from the author Gloria Galloway.

Printed in China

LIBRARY AND ARCHIVES CANADA CATALOGUING IN
PUBLICATION

Sanders, Moira, 1972–
     Harrow Fair : prize-winning recipes inspired by Canada's
favourite country fair / Moira Sanders & Lori Elstone with
Beth Goslin Maloney.

Includes index.
ISBN 978-1-77050-020-4

     1. Cookery. 2. Canning and preserving. I. Elstone, Lori,
1974– II. Goslin Maloney, Beth III. Title.

TX714.S325 2010   641.5   C2010-902258-0

The publisher acknowledges the financial support of the Government of Canada through the Canada Book Fund (CBF) and
the Province of British Columbia through the Book Publishing
Tax Credit.

10 11 12 13 14   5 4 3 2 1

this cookbook is dedicated to our children

GAVIN SANDERS, ELLEN SANDERS,

HUGH ELSTONE, ERICA ELSTONE,

& PATRICK MALONEY

&

to those who help make the
harrow fair so special

CONTENTS

FOREWORD

by Anna Olson

I love a good country fair, and have been to many in my lifetime. A visit to a fair is different than your Saturday morning trip to the farmers' market. Farmers' markets are very much about visiting with friends and neighbours over a stand of peach baskets brimming with Red Havens, and snacking on a grilled sausage on a bun at 8 a.m. while deciding you have time to make pickles out of the cucumbers you just bought.

A fair can encompass these things too—but a fair has its own energy and excitement that set it apart.

It's all about family. Activities abound at a fair for all generations, and you travel in groups, parking in a straw-strewn field as you march to the entrance expectantly. The kids rush ahead wanting to ride the ponies, while Mom carries her jars of jam for the preserve competition and Dad pushes the stroller with the wee one who has already managed to get apple cider over every inch of herself. A day at the fair disappears in a heartbeat, and everyone departs full, sleepy, and happy.

I do not need to touch on the activities that fill the day at the fair, because Lori and Moira have done so perfectly in *The Harrow Fair Cookbook*. This book is a perfect day at the fair, and you will feel that you have had the insider's tour from two lovely ladies whom you will feel are friends.

I am privileged to say that Lori and Moira are indeed friends of mine—I have known them for about 12 years now. There's yet to be a visit where we don't fall into peals of laughter over something inconsequential. And it is sheer joy to witness their passion for cooking and for family. Their hearts are so connected to Essex County, to their family roots, and to the need to share the traditions that give country fairs their worth, and I admire and respect those qualities that are so effortlessly ingrained in them.

Lori and Moira get a Red Ribbon in my book, and are most deserving of it.

See you at the Fair!

PIE AUCTION • PARADE

LIVE BANDS

CRAFT EXHIBITIONS

HORSE SHOWS

LAWN TRACTOR RACING

POULTRY, RABBIT,

SWINE, & CATTLE BARNS

DEMONSTRATION BOOTHS

PIGEON-ROLLING CONTEST

ABOUT THIS COOKBOOK

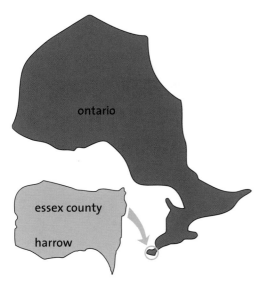

42°2´ N, 82°55´ W

WHERE THE HECK IS HARROW?

Harrow is located in Essex County, Ontario—the southernmost county in all of Canada. It, surprisingly, shares its latitude with northern California and the Tuscany region of Italy. A small peninsula of land quite literally jutting into the midwestern United States, Essex County is surrounded on three sides by water— Lake Erie to the south, the Detroit River to the west, and Lake St. Clair to the north.

Known as the "Sun Parlour of Canada," Essex County has long been a successful agricultural area thanks to its unique geographic location, temperate climate, long growing season, and clay-based soils. Harrow, with a population of just 3,000 people, is one of the smallest towns in the county, but it's also one of the most charming.

For the last 35 years, our parents have lived on Seymour Beach, located a few kilometres south of Harrow on the north shore of Lake Erie. Like Seymour, most local beaches were named after the families who farmed the land before it was sold for development. There are still dozens of orchards and fields stretching between Harrow and the lake, though—growing everything from apricots to zucchini. In the summer months, the picturesque stands of these farms overflow with an abundance of local fruits and vegetables.

DEEP ROOTS

Our family, the McDonalds, settled in Harrow in the late 1800s. While farming was a way of life for most local families at the time, it wasn't for ours. Our great-great-grandfather Hugh McDonald started one of the first Ford dealerships in Canada, which was eventually run by our grandfather, Edward. Papa was a savvy businessman who also served two terms as mayor of Harrow. His wife, Bertha, is a big reason why we both have food-focused careers. Grandma was an incredible cook and baker for her five children and eleven grandchildren.

A FAMILY (AF)FAIR

We're confident that six generations of the McDonald family have attended the Harrow Fair (officially dubbed the Colchester South and Harrow Agricultural Society Fair). Since its humble beginnings in 1854, when a few farmers gathered to trade livestock, seeds, and farm implements, the fair now attracts more than 70,000 visitors every Labour Day weekend. It is one of the oldest and most popular country fairs in all of Canada.

Our dad, Chuck McDonald (1943)

Moira's son, Gavin Sanders

Lori's son, Hugh Elstone

Growing up in Harrow, we took it for granted that we would attend the fair. As we got older, there were several years when we weren't able to be in town for the big event. After we started families of our own, though, we wanted to ensure our kids grew up experiencing the special magic of the Harrow Fair. Now we get together to watch the parade, explore the livestock exhibitions, marvel at the handmade crafts, chuckle at "bossy bingo," and cheer at the tractor pull. It's also great for catching up with extended family members and former schoolmates. Our uncle John McDonald has flown in from Vancouver to strut his stuff in the rooster-calling contest. And our friend Annie Lawton Scurfield, who now lives in New York City, makes the annual pilgrimage with her young family.

FOUR FUN-FILLED DAYS OF FAIR

The Harrow Fair takes place every Labour Day weekend. The fair organizers and volunteers do a tremendous job of putting together an amazingly diverse and complex event that really does have something for everyone. (We promise!) For more information about the history of the fair and details about next year's fair, please visit www.harrowfair.com.

FAIR COMPETITION

With our long-standing passion for cooking and baking, what we've come to love most about the Harrow Fair are its "Domestic Science" contests. When we began entering some of our creations a few years ago, we were surprised at the seriousness of the rules and the high calibre of the competition—but that's what makes participating such a fun challenge.

Seeing how much fun we were having—win or lose—our families and friends weren't about to be left on the sidelines. Our mom, Sharon McDonald, entered her crabapple jelly and won 1st prize. Our dad, Chuck McDonald, entered the "Men Only" category with his barbecue sauce and won 3rd prize (he remains hopeful for a 1st). Uncle John entered his pumpkin pie and received an honourable mention, which, we assured him, was nothing to sneeze at.

THE HARROW FAIR COOKBOOK

All the recipes in this cookbook were inspired by the Harrow Fair and the produce grown in our area. Some are 1st prize winners—like Buttermilk Biscuits and Rhubarb Custard Pie—but many are just great recipes collected from or inspired by our family, friends, and neighbours. All the recipes celebrate fresh ingredients that can be easily sourced from local farms, orchards, and gardens.

One of the main goals of the fair is to help people learn to do things for themselves. The rules are explicit—everything must be made from scratch. The recipes in *The Harrow Fair Cookbook* reflect this important tenet that stretches back more than 150 years. The recipes also call for ingredients that are as traditional, wholesome, and natural as possible.

One of our now-favourite categories at the fair is canning. Canning had once seemed so old-fashioned. A tiresome chore that would take away from precious daylight hours we thought would be better spent hanging out on the beach and getting up to no good. But eventually our mom convinced us to start canning our own tomato sauce using her favourite recipe. Until then, we had no idea how satisfying it would be to reach for our own jars in the middle of winter. We now think canning is very, very cool. The cookbook begins with chapters on preserving for good reason.

We hope you love making the recipes in *The Harrow Fair Cookbook* as much as we've loved collecting, creating, and testing them.

COOKBOOK CRITERIA

During the writing of this cookbook, several criteria for selecting food helped shape its contents. These are the same criteria that guide us when selecting food for our family and friends.

LOCAL & SEASONAL PRODUCE

In recent years there has been a huge increase in consumer demand to eat more locally produced foods. The "locavore" movement has helped make shoppers aware that there are food choices available beyond those in the grocery store.

We're biased, but we believe Essex County is one of the best places in Canada to eat locally. The bounty of the area is truly staggering. In the spring, summer, and fall, farm stands overflow with fruits and vegetables grown in the fields, orchards, and greenhouses that lie just steps away.

Being in such close proximity to our food really allows local residents to eat produce that is perfectly ripe and in season. But sometimes there can be too much seasonal bounty. (Anyone who has ever grown zucchini knows what we're talking about.) At other times, local availability is all too short. The apricot, for example, is at its sweet, juicy peak of perfection for only a few short weeks in the summer. While we try to make the most of this delicious fruit while it's in season, we want to be able to enjoy it year-round. As such, we would much rather make a batch of apricot jam (page 4) and freeze a few pounds of halved apricots than buy apricots shipped in from the southern hemisphere in January (which inevitably taste like cardboard).

So, preserving local fruits and vegetables for later use goes hand-in-hand with eating locally. The Preserving Summer Fruit and Preserving Summer Vegetables chapters contain great recipes and ideas for making everything from bumbleberry jam to tomato sauce.

NATURAL, TRADITIONAL, & UNPROCESSED FOOD

In a perfect world, we would use only organic ingredients in our recipes. Simply put, organic foods are grown on farms that work without the use of manufactured chemicals. This makes them better for our environment and our health. But while our organic choices are expanding every day, they're still not always available. So we try to make the best decisions we can, selecting ingredients that are as natural, traditional, and unprocessed as possible. Virtually all our recipes call for these types of ingredients. Eggs should come in shells, not pre-beaten in cartons. Vanilla should be made from vanilla beans, not flavoured wood pulp. You get the idea.

Fortunately, there are also several ingredients—ones we would have avoided calling for in the past—that are now available in more natural or organic versions, including vegetable shortening and corn syrup. (Candy making just isn't the same without corn syrup, trust us.)

MODERN TECHNIQUES

As much as we cherish traditional recipes and ingredients, we're not always keen on employing traditional, time-consuming cooking and baking techniques. We're realistic—and we're busy. So while we love making our Pear Cinnamon Twists, we'd much rather spend time with our families than spend a lot of time hand-kneading dough. We've come to consider our stand mixers, food processors, and blenders (classic and immersion) to be equipment essentials in our kitchens.

MODERATION

There are many recipes in this cookbook that are downright decadent. Hand-Cut Fries. Apple Fritter Rings. Cream Pie. Double-Double Chocolate Cake. Strawberry Shortcake Ice Cream. Okay, heaps of the recipes in this cookbook are downright decadent. But we aren't suggesting that anyone should be making and eating all these sweet treats on a daily basis. This cookbook is a collection of fun, delicious recipes that reflect summer, family get-togethers, and the Harrow Fair. Many of our recipes are meant to be special treats, and moderation is what makes a treat a treat.

PRESERVING SUMMER FRUIT

JAMS

pear jam

apricot jam

bumbleberry jam

sour cherry jam

tomato jam

SAUCES

blushing applesauce

strawberry sauce

over-the-top cherry sauce

CUT FRUIT

peach halves

BACK-TO-BASICS CANNING

Canning isn't difficult, and the results are so, so worth every bit of effort. But canning can be a little confusing if you're trying it for the first time. We suggest becoming familiar with the following details before starting any canning project. These basic pointers apply to almost all canning recipes.

To achieve the best canned goods, it's essential to use ripe fruits and vegetables.

PREPARING THE EQUIPMENT Assemble all required canning equipment, including a boiling water canner and canning jars, sealing lids, and rings (also known as screwbands), before you begin. Use heavy-bottomed stainless steel or hard-anodized aluminum pots and pans to cook your preserves before canning. Avoid any equipment made of copper, iron, zinc, or brass, as these materials may react with the ingredients and cause undesirable colour and taste changes, particularly in pickles.

PREPARING THE JARS Canning jars and lids must be prepared according to the manufacturer's directions. Always prepare one or two more jars than the recipe specifies. Sometimes jars break, and sometimes more jars are needed.

STERILIZING THE JARS First, wash all jars and rings in hot soapy water or run them through a cycle in the dishwasher. Then place the jars in the rack of the canner, cover them with water, and bring to a boil for 15 minutes. Leave the jars in the covered pot of hot water until you are ready to fill them.

PREPARING THE LIDS To sterilize the jar lids and soften the sealing compound, place them in a small pot of water and boil for 5 minutes. Leave the lids in the covered pot while you fill the jars. Always use new lids (they are not reusable).

FILLING THE JARS A wide-mouth funnel makes the job of filling jars easy and helps avoid mess. Complete the following steps for one jar before moving on to the next. Remove a sterilized jar from the hot water and fill, allowing headspace of ¼ to ½ inch (6 to 10 mm) between the contents of the jar and lid. Remove any air bubbles before sealing by gently tapping the jar on the counter or running a plastic knife or spatula around the inside of the jar.

Wipe away any drips from the top of the jar with a clean cloth. Place a prepared lid on the jar and apply a ring, gently tightened.

PROCESSING IN A BOILING WATER CANNER To prevent spoilage, a boiling water canner is essential for canning. A boiling water canner is a large pot (usually aluminum) fitted with a metal rack insert. Fill the canner about half full of water and bring to a boil while preparing the jars. Reduce the heat to medium and continue to simmer. Carefully place the hot, filled jars in the metal rack. Make sure all of the jars are fully submerged and bring the water back up to a boil. Once the water has returned to a boil, start the timer for the number of minutes indicated in the recipe.

COOLING THE JARS When finished processing, carefully remove all of the jars from the hot water.

The heat from the cooked contents should seal the lids within 1 hour. The first indication that the jars have sealed is the distinctive "pop" sound that each lid will make as it is sucked down by the force of the vacuum created by the heat inside the jar. To check that the jars have sealed properly, press on the lid. If the lid doesn't move, the jar is sealed and airtight. If a jar does not seal, place it in the refrigerator and consume within a few months.

Allow the jars to cool on a counter for 24 hours before moving.

After 24 hours, gently retighten the lids.

STORING THE JARS Store the canned items in a cool, dark place. Virtually all canned items will keep for up to 1 year until the next canning season.

pear jam

Lori had the good fortune (and good sense) to marry into a family of good cooks. The Lethby family's recipe is the inspiration for this exceptional pear jam. It has a gentle flavour with just a hint of spice. Makes three 8 oz (250 mL) jars.

5½ cups (1.375 L) peeled, cored, and
   chopped fresh pears
2 Tbsp (30 mL) fresh lemon juice
1½ cups (375 mL) granulated sugar
1 cinnamon stick, about 3 inches
   (8 cm) in length

**THE
HARROW
FAIR**
—
authors'
FAVE

Prepare three 8 oz (250 mL) jars, lids, and rings for canning (see Back-to-Basics Canning, facing page). Hold the sterilized jars in the boiling water canner until needed.

Place the pears and lemon juice in a large stockpot. Add the sugar. Let the mixture sit at room temperature for 1 hour until the sugar is mostly dissolved, stirring occasionally.

Add the cinnamon stick and bring the mixture to a boil over medium-high heat, stirring often, until the sugar is totally dissolved. Simmer the jam over medium heat, continuing to stir often, for 20 minutes or until the jam thickens and runs off the side of a spoon in heavy drops. Remove from heat. Skim off any foam that rises to the surface of the jam. Remove the cinnamon stick.

Fill and seal the hot jars one at a time, according to the manufacturer's directions. Process the jars in the boiling water canner for 10 minutes.

STORAGE   Enjoy at any point, but use within 1 year.

apricot jam

The season for apricots is short, lasting only a few weeks in August. Pick up apricots at a local farm stand and make them last all year by making this fabulous jam.

Makes three 8 oz (250 mL) jars.

5½ cups (1.375 L) chopped and pitted fresh apricots
2 Tbsp (30 mL) fresh lemon juice
1½ cups (375 mL) granulated sugar

Prepare three 8 oz (250 mL) jars, lids, and rings for canning (see Back-to-Basics Canning, page 2). Hold the sterilized jars in the boiling water canner until needed.

Place the apricots and lemon juice in a large stockpot. Add the sugar. Let the mixture sit at room temperature for 1 hour until the sugar is mostly dissolved, stirring occasionally.

Bring the mixture to a boil over medium-high heat, stirring often. Simmer the jam over medium heat, continuing to stir often, for 20 minutes or until the jam thickens and runs off the side of a spoon in heavy drops. Remove from heat. Skim off any foam that rises to the surface of the jam.

Fill and seal the hot jars one at a time, according to the manufacturer's directions. Process the jars in the boiling water canner for 10 minutes.

STORAGE Enjoy at any point, but use within 1 year.

▶ Jam is summer in a jar. Our favourite jams are made from simple, natural ingredients: fruit, sugar, and a touch of lemon juice. Well-made jam tastes like fruit (not sugar), is brightly coloured, and has a soft, spreadable consistency.

Most jam recipes call for the addition of commercially made pectin, which is available in liquid or powdered form. The truth is, commercial pectin isn't needed to make great jam. Pectin is a carbohydrate that naturally occurs in all fruits, in varying amounts. It helps to bind cell walls together, so it helps jam to gel. Almost all fruit will set properly for jam if it is correctly prepared and cooked.

If you go through jam quickly in your household, it's not necessary to seal any of our jam recipes in jars. (Canning is intended for storing jam for up to 1 year.) Instead, the jams can be stored in the refrigerator in airtight containers for up to 3 months.

Fruit for jam should be chopped according to personal preference. If a chunky jam is preferred, cut the fruit into large pieces. If a smooth jam is preferred, finely chop the fruit. While the jam is cooking, a potato masher can also be used to further crush the fruit.

bumbleberry jam

We like to think of bumbleberries as a jumbly, bumbly mix of any ripe, in-season berries. Makes three 8 oz (250 mL) jars.

3 cups (750 mL) hulled and chopped
    fresh strawberries
3 Tbsp (45 mL) fresh lemon juice
1½ cups (375 mL) granulated sugar
1¼ cups (310 mL) fresh blueberries
1¼ cups (310 mL) fresh raspberries

Prepare three 8 oz (250 mL) jars, lids, and rings for canning (see Back-to-Basics Canning, page 2). Hold the sterilized jars in the boiling water canner until needed.

Place the strawberries, lemon juice, and sugar in a large stockpot. Let the mixture sit at room temperature for 1 hour until the sugar is mostly dissolved, stirring occasionally.

Bring the mixture to a boil over medium-high heat, stirring often, until the sugar is totally dissolved. Stir in the blueberries and raspberries. Simmer the jam over medium heat, continuing to stir often, for 20 minutes or until the jam thickens and runs off the side of a spoon in heavy drops. Skim off any foam that rises to the surface of the jam.

Fill and seal the hot jars one at a time, according to the manufacturer's directions. Process the jars in the boiling water canner for 10 minutes.

STORAGE   Enjoy at any point, but use within 1 year.

▶ RASPBERRY JAM   To make raspberry jam, simply substitute 6 cups (1.5 L) of raspberries (for all the berries) and follow the directions above, omitting the addition of more fruit halfway through.

sour cherry jam

Our cousin Beth would have never forgiven us if we didn't include this jam in the cookbook. Sour cherries are the apple of her eye. Makes three 8 oz (250 mL) jars.

6 cups (1.5 L) pitted fresh sour
    cherries, divided
3 Tbsp (45 mL) fresh lemon juice
1½ cups (375 mL) granulated sugar

Prepare three 8 oz (250 mL) jars, tops, and rings for canning (see Back-to-Basics Canning, page 2). Hold the sterilized jars in the boiling water canner until needed.

Chop 4 cups (1 L) of the cherries in a food processor until almost smooth.

Place the chopped cherries, the 2 cups (500 mL) whole cherries, lemon juice, and sugar in a large stockpot. Let the mixture sit at room temperature for 1 hour until the sugar is mostly dissolved, stirring occasionally.

Bring the mixture to a boil over medium-high heat, stirring often, until the sugar is totally dissolved. Simmer the jam over medium heat, continuing to stir often, for 20 minutes or until the jam runs off the side of a spoon in heavy drops. Skim off any foam that rises to the surface of the jam.

Fill and seal the hot jars one at a time. Process the jars in the boiling water canner for 10 minutes.

STORAGE Enjoy at any point, but use within 1 year.

▶ If sour cherries are not in season, substitute with 4 cups (1 L) frozen sour cherries (thawed) and 2 cups (500 mL) sour cherry juice. Chop 3 cups (750 mL) of the cherries in a food processor, then add the juice when the remaining 1 cup (250 mL) of whole cherries is added to the stockpot.

tomato jam

The inspiration for this jam came from the John R. Park Homestead's cookbook. This recipe treats tomatoes like a fruit (which they technically are, as they come from flowering plants and contain seeds). The jam is as delicious as it is unique. Serve it at a special breakfast with warm buttermilk biscuits (page 36). Makes three 8 oz (250 mL) jars.

3 cups (750 mL) peeled and coarsely chopped fresh tomatoes (see note on page 24)
2 Tbsp (30 mL) fresh lemon juice
2 cups (500 mL) granulated sugar
1 tsp (5 mL) lemon zest
1 cinnamon stick, about 3 inches (8 cm) in length

Toss together the tomatoes, lemon juice, and sugar in a large bowl. Let the mixture sit at room temperature for at least 4 hours or overnight, stirring occasionally until the sugar is mostly dissolved.

Prepare three 8 oz (250 mL) jars, tops, and rings for canning (see Back-to-Basics Canning, page 2).

Place the tomato mixture in a sieve, and strain the juice into a large stockpot. Set aside the tomatoes.

Bring the juice to a boil over medium-high heat, stirring often, until the sugar is totally dissolved. Simmer the juice over medium heat for 30 minutes or until the juice starts to thicken.

Stir in the tomatoes, lemon zest, and cinnamon stick.

Bring the ingredients back up to a boil. Simmer the jam over medium heat, continuing to stir often, for another 30 minutes or until the jam runs off the side of a spoon in heavy drops. Skim off any foam that rises to the surface of the jam. Remove the cinnamon stick.

Fill and seal the hot jars one at a time. Process the jars in the boiling water canner for 10 minutes.

STORAGE Enjoy at any point, but use within 1 year.

▶ Built in 1842, John R. Park Homestead is a working example of life in southwestern Ontario as it was in the mid-19th century. Today, visitors can tour the stately main house, taste baked goods made in the original kitchen, participate in the harvesting of maple syrup, or simply enjoy the beautiful view of Lake Erie.

The picturesque homestead is located along the north shore of Lake Erie, between Kingsville and Harrow.

blushing applesauce

Our maternal grandfather, Ken Smith, was one of the sweetest people we've ever known. It's fitting that his specialty in the kitchen was applesauce. We can still picture him cranking the arm of his apple corer while he talked to us about his latest activities (which included woodworking, mandolin playing, and square dancing). His secret was adding the red skins of apples to the sauce while it was cooking so it would turn pink.

Makes about four 8 oz (250 mL) jars.

12 large red-skinned apples
½ cup (125 mL) water

Prepare four 8 oz (250 mL) jars, tops, and rings for canning (see Back-to-Basics Canning, page 2). Hold the sterilized jars in the boiling water canner until needed.

Wash the apples thoroughly.

Quarter the apples and remove the cores. Roughly chop the apples. Place the chopped apples and water in a large stockpot. Cook over medium heat for 30 minutes or until the apples soften and become sauce.

Push the sauce through a strainer or food mill to remove the skins.

Fill and seal the hot jars one at a time, according to the manufacturer's directions. Process the jars in the boiling water canner for 20 minutes.

STORAGE Enjoy at any point, but use within 1 year.

▶ Instead of canning, you can just keep the applesauce in your refrigerator. The applesauce can also be frozen for up to 3 months.

The red-skinned varieties that work best in this applesauce are Cortland, Empire, and McIntosh.

▶ SUGAR & SPICE BLUSHING APPLESAUCE Add ¼ cup (60 mL) brown sugar, ¼ tsp (1 mL) ground cinnamon, and a pinch of grated nutmeg to the apples while they are cooking.

strawberry sauce

Essex County has the first ripe strawberries in all of Canada but, like everywhere, the season is too short! This sauce really captures the flavour of fresh, ripe strawberries. If it's frozen for later use, it will remind everyone of summer long after strawberries have finished for the season. Makes 2 cups (500 mL).

3 cups (750 mL) hulled fresh
     strawberries
1 cup (250 mL) granulated sugar
¼ cup (60 mL) fresh lemon juice

Chop the strawberries, sugar, and lemon juice in a food processor until smooth. If the sauce is too thick, dilute it with a small amount of water.

STORAGE The sauce can be used right away or stored in an airtight container in the refrigerator for up to 2 weeks. It can also be frozen in containers, but should be used within 6 months.

▶ Try this sauce in homemade strawberry sundaes, made with frozen custard (page 210) and whipped cream (page 171).

over-the-top cherry sauce

What makes this sauce over-the-top is the addition of the seeds scraped from a vanilla bean. Vanilla beans are a bit expensive, but they're worth it for the depth of flavour they add to this sauce. Serve over Vanilla Bean Cheesecake (page 180). Makes 2 cups (500 mL).

3 cups (750 mL) pitted fresh sour
    cherries
½ cup (125 mL) granulated sugar
2 Tbsp (30 mL) fresh lemon juice
2 Tbsp (30 mL) cornstarch
½ vanilla bean

Mix together the cherries and sugar in a medium saucepan set over medium heat.

Mix the lemon juice and cornstarch together in a small bowl.

When the cherries begin to bubble, add the cornstarch mixture. Cook, stirring occasionally, for 5 minutes or until the sauce thickens enough to coat a spoon.

Cut the vanilla lengthwise in half and scrape out the seeds using the back of a knife. Stir the seeds into the sauce until incorporated (save the scraped-out vanilla bean for another use). Remove the pan from the heat and set aside to cool.

STORAGE The sauce can be used as soon as it's cool, but can also be stored in an airtight container in the refrigerator for up to 2 weeks.

▶ The seeds of the vanilla bean can be replaced with 1 tsp (5 mL) pure vanilla extract.

Instead of discarding the vanilla bean after the seeds have been removed, place it in a sugar bowl. It will delicately perfume the sugar.

peach halves

Peach halves are a great item to have in your pantry. They are both an instant snack and a dessert. We've specified how many peaches to use, but it's really easy to make as many jars as there are peaches. A 32 oz (1 L) jar holds seven to eight peaches, depending on their size. Makes four 32 oz (1 L) jars.

1⅓ cups (330 mL) granulated sugar
1⅓ cups (330 mL) water
32 fresh peaches, peeled, pitted,
    and halved

Prepare four 32 oz (1 L) jars, lids, and rings for canning (see Back-to-Basics Canning, page 2). Hold the sterilized jars in the boiling water canner until needed.

Place ⅓ cup (80 mL) sugar and ⅓ cup (80 mL) water in each jar. Swirl the sugar in the jars until it is mostly dissolved.

Pack each jar with peach halves until nearly full. Place a large peach half sideways in the opening of each jar. (This will anchor everything in place and prevent the peaches from floating to the top of the jar.) Fill each jar with additional water, leaving ½ inch (1 cm) of space at the top. Gently tap each jar to release any air bubbles.

Seal the jars according to the manufacturer's directions. Process the jars in the boiling water canner for 30 minutes.

STORAGE Enjoy at any point, but use within 1 year.

▶ PEELING PEACHES Bring a large pot of water to boil. Prepare an ice water bath by filling a large bowl with cold water and a few cups of ice. Score an X into the bottom of each peach. Place the peaches in the boiling water. Remove after 1 minute or when parts of the skin begin to curl. Transfer the peaches to the ice water bath. Repeat the process with all the peaches. After the peaches have cooled for a few minutes, the skins will easily peel off. Cut each peach in half and remove the pit. Place in a bowl of cold water along with the juice of 1 lemon, until ready to can.

THE DEEP FREEZE

Freezing fruit is an excellent way to enjoy summer's sweet harvest all year. Follow these steps for best results:

1. Select fruit that is perfectly ripe but still slightly firm.
2. Wash fruit thoroughly.
3. Prepare the fruit (see below).
4. Line a baking sheet with a piece of parchment paper.
5. Arrange the fruit on a baking sheet so the pieces aren't touching. This helps the fruit keep its shape and prevents it from freezing together in a giant clump. This method is known as individual quick freezing (IQF).
6. Place the baking sheet in the freezer until the fruit is frozen solid.
7. Transfer the frozen fruit to plastic containers or freezer bags.
8. Keep the fruit frozen until ready to use.

PREPARING FRUIT FOR FREEZING

APRICOTS, NECTARINES, PEACHES, & PLUMS Remove skins, if desired. Cut into halves or quarters.

BLACKBERRIES, BLUEBERRIES, & RASPBERRIES Leave whole.

CHERRIES Pit. Leave whole.

RHUBARB Cut into 2-inch (5 cm) pieces.

STRAWBERRIES Hull. Leave whole or cut into halves or quarters.

PRESERVING SUMMER VEGETABLES

CONDIMENTS & SAUCES

basil pesto

herb pesto

red onion marmalade

mustard relish

vegetable salsa

barbecue sauce

tomato & basil sauce

one stop tomato sauce

VEGETABLES

dill pickles

bread & butter pickles

pickled asparagus

pickled beets

chopped tomatoes

basil pesto

Most people think of pesto in the traditional sense, as a sauce for pastas like linguine and fettuccine. But it's also fab when used as a condiment. Try it on a Tomato, Mozzarella, & Pesto Sandwich (page 113). Makes 2 cups (500 mL).

4 cups (1 L) firmly packed fresh basil
½ cup (125 mL) pine nuts
2 garlic cloves, peeled
1 tsp (5 mL) fine sea salt
1 cup (250 mL) extra virgin olive oil
½ cup (125 mL) grated Parmesan
    cheese

Finely chop the basil, pine nuts, garlic, and salt in a food processor. Pour in the olive oil in a slow, steady stream while the motor is still running.

Add the cheese and pulse until combined.

Add more olive oil, if necessary, to achieve a thick, smooth consistency.

STORAGE This pesto is at its best when freshly made, but when topped with a thin layer of extra virgin olive oil it will keep in the refrigerator for up to 1 week.

It can also be frozen for up to 6 months.

▶ For a lighter but still excellent version of basil pesto, simply omit the pine nuts and cheese.

herb pesto

This pesto is a fragrant, flavourful emulsion made from common summer herbs that tastes anything but common. Experiment with it to see how it can enhance dishes like Seven-Strata Salad (page 103) and Buttered Pickerel (page 134). Makes 2 cups (500 mL).

2 cups (500 mL) firmly packed
    fresh curly-leaf parsley
1 cup (250 mL) firmly packed
    fresh dill
1 cup (250 mL) firmly packed
    fresh chives
1 tsp (5 mL) fine sea salt
¼ cup (60 mL) fresh lemon juice
1 cup (250 mL) extra virgin olive oil

Finely chop the parsley, dill, chives, and salt in a food processor. Add the lemon juice and pulse until combined. Pour in the olive oil in a slow, steady stream while the motor is still running.

Add more olive oil, if necessary, to achieve a thick, smooth consistency.

STORAGE This pesto is at its best when freshly made, but when topped with a thin layer of extra virgin olive oil it will keep in the refrigerator for up to 1 week.

It can also be frozen for up to 6 months.

red onion marmalade

Something wonderful happens to the red onions when they are cooked with vinegar and sugar. They lose their sharpness and become softer, sweeter versions of themselves. This easy-to-make recipe will become an essential condiment in your refrigerator. Try it with a roast beef sandwich (page 109) or as a topping on your next hamburger (page 121). Makes 1½ cups (375 mL).

3 cups (750 mL) thinly sliced
    red onion
1 cup (250 mL) white vinegar
1 cup (250 mL) granulated sugar

Combine all ingredients in a small saucepan set over medium-low heat. Cook for 30 minutes or until the onions are soft and the marmalade has become syrupy.

STORAGE   Store in an airtight container in the refrigerator for up to 1 month.

mustard relish

This recipe was passed down from our great-great-aunt, Ila Quigley, to our grandma Lela Smith, to our mom, Sharon McDonald. In Aunt Ila's day, everything would have been chopped by hand. We're so much lazier now . . . Makes eight 16 oz (500 mL) jars.

8 cups (2 L) coarsely chopped
    pickling cucumbers
2 cups (500 mL) coarsely chopped
    sweet red pepper
2 cups (500 mL) coarsely chopped
    green pepper
½ cup (125 mL) pickling salt
6 cups (1.5 L) white vinegar
6 cups (1.5 L) granulated sugar
2 Tbsp (30 mL) turmeric
2 Tbsp (30 mL) celery seeds
¾ cup (185 mL) yellow mustard
¾ cup (185 mL) all-purpose flour

Place the vegetables in a large bowl. Sprinkle with pickling salt and mix thoroughly. Let the mixture sit at room temperature overnight.

The next day, prepare eight 16 oz (500 mL) jars, lids, and rings for canning (see Back-to-Basics Canning, page 2). Hold the sterilized jars in the boiling water canner until needed.

Place the vegetables in a large colander to drain off the liquid. Rinse with cold water.

Bring the vegetable mixture, vinegar, sugar, turmeric, and celery seeds to a boil in a large stockpot. Simmer over medium heat, stirring often, for 30 minutes or until the cucumbers are transparent.

Mix together the mustard and flour in a large bowl until smooth. Slowly add 3 cups (750 mL) of the hot vegetable mixture to the mustard and flour mixture, continuously whisking until well incorporated and smooth.

Pour this mixture back into the stockpot, stirring briskly to avoid lumps. Simmer over medium heat, stirring frequently, for 10 minutes or until creamy and opaque.

Fill and seal the hot jars one at a time, according to the manufacturer's directions. Process the jars in the boiling water canner for 15 minutes.

STORAGE Enjoy at any point, but use within 1 year.

▶ A food processor makes quick work of chopping vegetables. To prevent the vegetables from being too finely chopped, chop each type of vegetable separately.

▶ Essex County has more greenhouses per hectare than anywhere else in North America. The greenhouses employ the latest technology to help maximize their productivity, with astonishing results. Each greenhouse acre produces the equivalent of 64 acres (26 hectares) of conventionally grown vegetables. And the use of cutting-edge hydroponic and pest management techniques yields produce that is virtually organic.

Essex County greenhouse produce appears around the continent. We've had family members spot it in grocery stores from New York City to St. Barts in the Caribbean. The most popular crops? Specialty tomatoes, seedless cucumbers, and colourful sweet peppers.

vegetable salsa

This salsa has a lively, fresh taste and is great to have on hand in jars year-round. The recipe is from our friend Tara Meyer, who got it from Art Zitlau, the long-time principal of Harrow Senior Public School. Makes six 16 oz (500 mL) jars.

10 cups (2.5 L) chopped fresh
   tomatoes
2 cups (500 mL) chopped
   yellow onion
1½ cups (375 mL) seeded and finely
   chopped fresh jalapeño peppers
1 cup (250 mL) finely chopped green
   pepper
1 cup (250 mL) finely chopped celery
1 cup (250 mL) finely chopped carrots
4 red hot chili peppers, seeded and
   finely chopped
5 garlic cloves, minced
¾ cup (185 mL) white vinegar
1½ tsp (7 mL) ground cumin
½ cup (125 mL) tomato paste
¼ cup (60 mL) granulated sugar
2 Tbsp (30 mL) kosher salt
½ cup (125 mL) finely chopped
   fresh basil
½ cup (125 mL) finely chopped
   fresh cilantro
¼ cup (60 mL) fresh lime juice

Prepare six 16 oz (500 mL) jars, lids, and rings for canning (see Back-to-Basics Canning, page 2). Hold the sterilized jars in the boiling water canner until needed.

Place all of the chopped vegetables in a large stockpot. Stir in the vinegar, cumin, tomato paste, sugar, and salt. Bring the salsa to a boil, then simmer over medium-high heat for 30 minutes, stirring occasionally.

Stir in the basil, cilantro, and lime juice. Remove from the heat.

Fill and seal the hot jars one at a time, according to the manufacturer's directions. Process the jars in the boiling water canner for 15 minutes.

STORAGE   Enjoy at any point, but use within 1 year.

▶ If you are chopping hot peppers by hand, we recommend wearing plastic gloves. While working, be careful not to touch your face, especially your eyes.

THE
HARROW
FAIR

authors'
FAVE

barbecue sauce

This recipe is the creation of Lori's husband, Jake, who takes grilling very seriously. He made it everything a good barbecue sauce should be . . . smoky, spicy, tangy, and saucy.

Makes four 16 oz (500 mL) jars.

¼ cup (60 mL) vegetable oil
2 cups (500 mL) chopped
    yellow onion
6 garlic cloves, chopped
8 cups (2 L) chopped fresh tomatoes
1 tsp (5 mL) red chili flakes
4 tsp (20 mL) smoked paprika
1 cup (250 mL) firmly packed
    brown sugar
2 Tbsp (30 mL) Dijon mustard
2 cups (500 mL) Heinz ketchup
½ cup (125 mL) apple cider vinegar
2 tsp (10 mL) fine sea salt
1 tsp (5 mL) freshly ground
    black pepper

Prepare four 16 oz (500 mL) jars, lids, and rings for canning (see Back-to-Basics Canning, page 2). Hold the sterilized jars in the boiling water canner until needed.

Heat the oil in a large stockpot set over medium heat. Add the onion and cook for 5 minutes, or until softened.

Stir in the remaining ingredients. Bring to a boil then simmer over medium heat for 30 minutes, stirring occasionally.

Blend the sauce in a food processor until smooth. Return the sauce to the stockpot, and bring the sauce back up to a boil. Remove from heat.

Fill and seal the hot jars one at a time, according to the manufacturer's directions. Process the jars in the boiling water canner for 20 minutes.

STORAGE Enjoy at any point, but use within 1 year.

▶ This sauce can also be frozen (instead of canned) for up to 6 months in convenient 2-cup (500 mL) portions (the perfect amount for barbecued ribs, page 123).

tomato & basil sauce

No matter how many batches of this sauce we make in September, it's never enough to last us through the winter. Made with fresh tomatoes and basil, this is our go-to sauce for Eggplant Parm'wiches (page 140) or any meal where we need a simple but delicious tomato sauce. Makes eight 16 oz (500 mL) jars.

1 cup (250 mL) extra virgin olive oil

9 garlic cloves, peeled

18 cups (4.5 L) peeled and seeded fresh tomatoes (see notes on page 24), reserving 2 cups (500 mL) tomato water (see note, this page)

2 Tbsp (30 mL) fine sea salt

½ cup (125 mL) firmly packed fresh basil

Prepare eight 16 oz (500 mL) jars, lids, and rings for canning (see Back-to-Basics Canning, page 2). Hold the sterilized jars in the boiling water canner until needed.

Heat the oil in a large stockpot set over medium heat. Add the whole garlic cloves and cook over low heat for 5 minutes, or until they are softened.

Stir in the tomatoes and salt. Bring the sauce to a boil, then simmer over medium heat for 30 minutes, stirring occasionally.

Stir in the basil and the reserved tomato water. Blend the sauce in a food processor until smooth.

Return the sauce to the stockpot. Bring the sauce back up to a boil. Remove from heat.

Fill and seal the hot jars one at a time, according to the manufacturer's directions. Process the jars in the boiling water canner for 20 minutes.

STORAGE Enjoy at any point, but use within 1 year.

▶ Tomato water is the juice that is collected and saved from the process of seeding the tomatoes. To collect tomato water after you have finished seeding tomatoes, place the seeds and pulp in a fine sieve set over a large bowl.

one stop tomato sauce

When we were growing up on Seymour Beach near Colchester, the closest variety store was called The One Stop. It wasn't fancy, but it had pretty much everything we needed in a pinch. Same goes for this tomato sauce. The recipe is from our mom, who has been canning it for family and friends for years. Makes eight 16 oz (500 mL) jars.

16 cups (4 L) peeled and seeded
    fresh tomatoes (see notes)
3 cups (750 mL) chopped
    yellow onion
2 cups (500 mL) chopped celery
2 cups (500 mL) chopped fresh
    zucchini
1 cup (250 mL) chopped fresh
    green pepper
1 cup (250 mL) chopped fresh
    sweet red pepper
¼ cup (60 mL) minced garlic
2 Tbsp (30 mL) fine sea salt
2 Tbsp (30 mL) granulated sugar

THE
HARROW
FAIR

———

authors'
FAVE

Prepare eight 16 oz (500 mL) jars, lids, and rings for canning (see Back-to-Basics Canning, page 2). Hold the sterilized jars in the boiling water canner until needed.

Chop the tomatoes in a food processor until smooth. Place the pulp in a large stockpot. Stir in the onion, celery, zucchini, green pepper, red pepper, garlic, salt, and sugar.

Bring the sauce to a boil, then simmer over medium heat for 1 hour, stirring occasionally. Remove from heat.

Fill and seal the hot jars one at a time, according to the manufacturer's directions. Process the jars in the boiling water canner for 20 minutes.

STORAGE Enjoy at any point, but use within 1 year.

▶ PEELING TOMATOES Bring a large pot of water to a boil. Prepare an ice water bath by filling a large bowl with cold water and a few cups of ice. Cut off the core end and score an X into the bottom of each tomato. Place the tomatoes in the boiling water. Remove after 1 minute or when parts of the skin begin to curl. Transfer the tomatoes to the ice water bath. Repeat the process with all of the tomatoes. After the tomatoes have cooled for a few minutes, the skins will easily peel off.

▶ SEEDING TOMATOES After the tomatoes have been peeled, cut the tomatoes in half lengthwise. Squeeze each half into a bowl until the seeds come out. Remove any remaining seeds clinging to the tomato flesh.

dill pickles

This recipe is from Lori's mother-in-law, Roberta Parry. She showed us how she makes her pickles so now we have no excuse for not having enough jars in our pantries. We prefer pickles without garlic, but they are delicious either way. Makes six 32 oz (1 L) jars.

24 cups (6 L) fresh, unbruised pickling
    cucumbers, about 3 inches (8 cm)
    in length
12 cups (3 L) water
4 cups (1 L) pickling vinegar
½ cup (125 mL) pickling salt
6 large fresh dill heads
6 garlic cloves, peeled (optional)

THE
HARROW
FAIR

1st

Wash cucumbers thoroughly in cold water. Cover them completely in cold water and store overnight in the refrigerator.

The next day, prepare six 32 oz (1 L) jars, lids, and rings for canning (see Back-to-Basics Canning, page 2). Hold the sterilized jars in the boiling water canner until needed.

Place the cucumbers in a large colander to drain. Rinse with cold water.

Bring the water, vinegar, and salt to a boil in a large stockpot. Continue to simmer the brine over medium heat.

Fill 1 jar at a time with 1 dill head, 1 garlic clove (if using), and cucumbers (tightly packed). Pour the hot brine into the jars, leaving ½ inch (1 cm) headspace at the top. The pickles must be fully submerged in the hot brine.

Seal the hot jars, according to the manufacturer's directions. Process the jars in the boiling water canner for 20 minutes.

STORAGE Following Roberta's lead, we wait until Thanksgiving to open our pickles. Use within 1 year.

▶ PICKLE POINTERS
- Always use fresh pickling cucumbers (not salad cucumbers), which are widely available in July and August.
- Pickling vinegar contains 7 percent acidity, while conventional white vinegar typically contains only 5 percent acidity. Pickling vinegar is needed to make these pickles properly sour.
- Always use pickling salt, a natural ingredient. Other salts can contain iodine, a chemical that can darken pickles, or anti-caking agents that can cause cloudiness in the brine. Pickling salt acts as a preservative and adds flavour and crispness to pickles.
- Always use unblossomed dill heads for this recipe, rather than the feathery leaves of the dill plant.

▶ In Canada, a red ribbon is always awarded to a competitor finishing in first place; a blue ribbon is awarded to second-place finishers. In the United States, it's the reverse—a blue ribbon is for first place, and a red ribbon is for second place.

bread & butter pickles

Bread and butter pickles supposedly earned their name during the Great Depression. The sweet, tangy, and crunchy pickles were a staple because they were inexpensive and could become a meal when sandwiched between bread and butter. These days, they're an essential burger topping. Makes five 16 oz (500 mL) jars.

10 cups (2.5 L) fresh pickling
   cucumbers, cut into ¼-inch
   (6 mm) slices
3 cups (750 mL) thinly sliced
   white onion
½ cup (125 mL) pickling salt
3 cups (750 mL) pickling vinegar
2 cups (500 mL) granulated sugar
4 tsp (20 mL) mustard seeds
1 tsp (5 mL) celery seeds
1 tsp (5 mL) turmeric

Combine the sliced cucumbers, onions, and salt in a large bowl. Fill the bowl with cold water and mix well. Let the mixture sit at room temperature overnight.

The next day, prepare five 16 oz (500 mL) jars, lids, and rings for canning (see Back-to-Basics Canning, page 2). Hold the sterilized jars in the boiling water canner until needed.

Place the vegetables in a large colander to drain off the liquid. Rinse with cold water.

Bring the vinegar, sugar, mustard seeds, celery seeds, and turmeric to a boil in a large stockpot. Stir in the cucumbers and onions. Bring the mixture to a boil. Remove from heat.

Fill and seal the hot jars one at a time, according to the manufacturer's directions. Process the jars in the boiling water canner for 10 minutes.

STORAGE   Enjoy at any point, but use within 1 year.

THE
HARROW
FAIR
—
authors'
FAVE

pickled asparagus

For years, our uncle Tom Mallard grew asparagus in his fields, located just east of Harrow. Many bundles of asparagus made their way to our house for weeks every spring. Pickling was—and still is—a great way to preserve asparagus for later use. Try our pickled asparagus as a garnish in Bloody Good Caesars (page 58). Makes seven 32 oz (I L) jars.

6 lb (2.7 kg) fresh asparagus
8 cups (2 L) water
2 cups (500 mL) pickling vinegar
3 Tbsp (45 mL) pickling salt
7 fresh tarragon sprigs
21 black peppercorns

Prepare seven 32 oz (1 L) jars, lids, and rings for canning (see Back-to-Basics Canning, page 2). Hold the sterilized jars in the boiling water canner until needed.

Wash the asparagus thoroughly in cold water. Trim the ends to fit into the jars.

Bring the water, vinegar, and salt to a boil in a large stockpot. Continue to simmer the brine over medium heat.

Fill each jar with 1 tarragon sprig and 3 peppercorns. Tightly pack the asparagus, tips down, into the jars. Pour the hot brine into the jars, leaving ½ inch (1 cm) headspace at the top. The asparagus must be fully submerged in the hot brine.

Seal the hot jars, according to the manufacturer's directions. Process the jars in the boiling water canner for 20 minutes.

STORAGE   Store the asparagus for at least 1 month before enjoying it. Use within 1 year.

▸ Asparagus is the first official crop of spring. Essex County's asparagus season begins around May 1 and lasts for six weeks.

pickled beets

Pickled beets make a tasty, colourful addition to pickle trays, salads, and even burgers. Consider yourself forewarned . . . this is by far the messiest recipe in the book. Makes about five 16 oz (500 mL) jars.

5 lb (2.2 kg) fresh red beets
6 cups (1.5 L) apple cider vinegar
1½ cups (375 mL) water
1 cup (250 mL) granulated sugar
3 Tbsp (45 mL) pickling salt

Preheat the oven to 400°F (200°C).

Wash the beets. Trim the tops and roots, then place the beets on a large baking sheet. Bake for 1 hour, or until just tender. Set aside to cool for at least 10 minutes. Remove the skins by filling a pan with cold water and submerging the beets. The skins should slip off easily.

Prepare five 16 oz (500 mL) jars, lids, and rings for canning (see Back-to-Basics Canning, page 2). Hold the sterilized jars in the boiling water canner until needed.

Bring the vinegar, water, sugar, and salt to a boil in a large stockpot. Continue to simmer the brine over medium heat.

Working quickly, pack the roasted beets into 1 jar at a time. Pour the hot brine into the jars, leaving ½ inch (1 cm) headspace at the top. The beets must be fully submerged in the hot brine.

Seal the hot jars, according to the manufacturer's directions. Process the jars in the boiling water canner for 20 minutes.

STORAGE Store the beets for at least 1 month prior to enjoying. Use within 1 year.

▶ Smaller beets are best for canning as they can be left whole. Larger beets must be halved or quartered to fit into the jars.

chopped tomatoes

Chopped tomatoes are incredibly useful to have on hand at all times. Use them in dishes like Turkey Chili (page 132) or in homemade pasta sauces. Makes seven 16 oz (500 mL) jars.

14 cups (3.5 L) peeled and seeded
    fresh tomatoes
1¾ tsp (9 mL) fresh lemon juice
7 tsp (35 mL) fine sea salt
14 fresh basil leaves

Prepare seven 16 oz (500 mL) jars, lids, and rings for canning (see Back-to-Basics Canning, page 2). Hold the sterilized jars in the boiling water canner until needed.

Coarsely chop the peeled and seeded tomatoes into ½-inch (1 cm) pieces and set aside.

Place ¼ tsp (1 mL) lemon juice, 1 tsp (5 mL) salt, and 2 basil leaves into each jar. Fill each jar with the chopped tomatoes, leaving ½ inch (1 cm) headspace at the top. Gently tap each jar to release any air bubbles.

Seal the hot jars, according to the manufacturer's directions. Process the jars in the boiling water canner for 30 minutes.

STORAGE The tomatoes can be enjoyed at any time but should be used within 1 year.

▶ We like to use Roma tomatoes in this recipe. See the instructions for peeling and seeding tomatoes (page 24).

THE DEEP FREEZE

As with fruit, freezing vegetables preserves them long after the summer harvest. Follow these steps for best results:

1. Select ripe vegetables.
2. Wash vegetables thoroughly.
3. Prepare vegetables as desired (see below).
4. Bring a large pot of salted water to boil.
5. Prepare an ice water bath.
6. Blanch the vegetables for up to 3 minutes, until brightly coloured or slightly softened.
7. Plunge the vegetables into the ice water.
8. Drain and set aside.
9. Line a baking sheet with a piece of parchment paper.
10. Arrange the vegetables on the baking sheet so they aren't touching.
11. Place the baking sheet in the freezer until the vegetables are frozen solid.
12. Transfer the frozen vegetables into containers or freezer bags.
13. Keep the vegetables frozen until ready to use.

PREPARING VEGETABLES FOR FREEZING

ASPARAGUS Remove woody ends. Cut into 2-inch (5 cm) pieces.

BEANS Remove stems.

BROCCOLI Cut florets into bite-sized pieces.

BRUSSELS SPROUTS Remove woody ends. Cut in half.

CARROTS Peel and slice into ¼-inch (6 mm) coins.

CAULIFLOWER Cut florets into bite-sized pieces.

SWEET CORN Cut kernels from the cob.

SWEET PEAS Shell.

BREAKFAST

SAVOURY

buttermilk biscuits

asparagus bread pudding

poached eggs with swiss
    chard

sweet corn fritters with
    peameal bacon

garden vegetable frittata

SWEET

oatmeal breakfast cookies

summer fruit salad

banana muffins

raspberry & lemon muffins

blueberry sour cream
    coffee cake

currant & maple scones

pear cinnamon twists

peachy french toast

zucchini bread

apple & oatmeal pancakes

buttermilk biscuits

Year after year, Carrie Piper-Hedges wins red ribbons for her buttermilk biscuits at the Harrow Fair. They come out perfectly every time. Makes 12 biscuits.

2 cups (500 mL) all-purpose flour
2 tsp (10 mL) baking powder
½ tsp (2 mL) baking soda
½ tsp (2 mL) fine sea salt
¼ cup (60 mL) vegetable shortening
    (or cold butter, cubed)
1 cup (250 mL) buttermilk (approx)
    (see note on page 49)

Preheat the oven to 450°F (230°C). Line a large baking sheet with parchment paper.

Sift together the flour, baking powder, baking soda, and salt in a large bowl. Working quickly and using a light touch, incorporate the shortening with your fingers or a pastry cutter until the largest pieces are the size of peas.

Add the buttermilk, stirring until the dough leaves the side of the bowl. The dough should be slightly sticky. If the dough is too dry, add up to 2 Tbsp (30 mL) buttermilk.

Knead the dough on a lightly floured board, 5 times or until the dough just comes together. Roll out the dough, using a floured rolling pin, to a thickness of ¾ inch (2 cm). Cut dough into 2-inch (5 cm) rounds with a biscuit cutter or a straight-sided glass.

Transfer the biscuits to the baking sheet, making sure the biscuits don't touch. Bake for 12 minutes or until the biscuits begin to turn golden.

Serve warm.

asparagus bread pudding

This is the perfect dish to serve to a brunch crowd. We make it for family and friends every spring, once local asparagus is in season. Serves 6.

3 cups (750 mL) fresh asparagus, cut into 3-inch (8 cm) pieces

1½ cups (375 mL) shredded Swiss cheese

1 cup (250 mL) grated Parmesan cheese

¼ cup (60 mL) chopped fresh chives

¼ cup (60 mL) chopped fresh flat-leaf parsley

1 Tbsp (15 mL) chopped fresh thyme

6 large eggs

1½ cups (375 mL) milk

1 tsp (5 mL) fine sea salt

¼ tsp (1 mL) freshly ground black pepper

8 cups (2 L) cubed day-old baguette (1-inch/2.5 cm cubes)

THE
HARROW
FAIR

authors'
FAVE

Bring a large pot of salted water to a boil, and prepare an ice water bath (see note on page 12). Blanch the asparagus in the boiling water for 3 minutes, then plunge it into the ice water. Drain the asparagus and set aside.

Combine the cheeses and herbs in a large bowl. Whisk together the eggs, milk, salt, and pepper in a separate bowl.

Arrange half of the bread in the bottom of an 8- × 8-inch (20 × 20 cm) baking pan. Cover the bread with half the asparagus, then half the cheese mixture, then half the egg mixture.

Continue with a second layer of bread cubes, asparagus, cheese mixture, and egg mixture. The pan will be very full, but it will fit.

Rest the pan at room temperature for 30 minutes.

Preheat the oven to 350°F (180°C). Bake for 45 minutes or until golden brown.

Serve warm.

▷ This recipe really benefits from quality cheeses. Most local grocery stores now stock cheeses once found only in specialty food stores. For the Swiss cheese, we recommend Gruyère or Emmentaler; for the Parmesan cheese we recommend Parmigiano-Reggiano.

▷ When it comes to using fresh herbs in the recipes in this book, there are no substitutes. Dried herbs simply don't yield the intended results.

poached eggs with swiss chard

We've swapped Swiss chard for spinach in this perennially popular breakfast dish. Hollandaise sauce can be daunting. But if you know how to use a whisk, you can make this recipe. Serves 4.

SWISS CHARD

2 Tbsp (30 mL) unsalted butter
10 cups (2.5 L) loosely packed Swiss chard, stems removed
½ tsp (2 mL) fine sea salt
¼ tsp (1 mL) freshly ground black pepper

HOLLANDAISE SAUCE

6 large egg yolks
½ cup (125 mL) water
½ tsp (2 mL) fine sea salt
¼ tsp (1 mL) freshly ground black pepper
½ cup (125 mL) unsalted butter, softened
2 Tbsp (30 mL) fresh lemon juice

POACHED EGGS

1 Tbsp (15 mL) white vinegar
8 large eggs

4 large slices rustic white bread, toasted
Finely chopped fresh chives

SWISS CHARD

Melt the butter in a large stockpot set over medium heat. Add the chard and cook for 3 minutes or until the leaves begin to wilt. Season with salt and pepper.

Cover the pot with a lid and keep warm over low heat until needed.

HOLLANDAISE SAUCE

Whisk together the yolks, water, salt, and pepper in a saucepan.

Continue whisking over medium-low heat for 5 minutes or until the mixture is thick enough to coat the back of a spoon. Remove the sauce from the heat.

Whisk in the butter and lemon juice. Cover the pot with a lid to keep it warm.

POACHED EGGS

Bring a saucepan of water to a boil. Add 1 Tbsp (15 mL) white vinegar and reduce the heat to medium. Crack an egg into a small bowl and slip the egg into the simmering water. Add the other eggs in the same manner, without crowding the pan, and cook each egg between 2 and 3 minutes, depending on the preferred level of doneness. Keep track of the eggs: first in, first out is the rule. Remove the eggs from the pot and drain them on a plate lined with paper towels until needed.

ASSEMBLY

Set out 4 plates.

Place a toasted slice of rustic bread on each plate and top each with some Swiss chard and 2 poached eggs. Spoon the sauce over the eggs. Sprinkle with chopped chives.

▶ There are more than 80 chicken breeds shown at the Harrow Fair each year. Some have very intriguing names, such as Silver Laced Wyandotte, Blue Cochin, and Bearded Silkie.

▶ Swiss chard is a leafy vegetable that is similar to spinach in appearance and taste but is actually related to the garden beet. Its cooked leaves and stalks have a refined and delicate flavour, which makes it perfect for this dish.

sweet corn fritters with peameal bacon

Served with thin slices of peameal bacon and ripe beefsteak tomatoes, these Sweet Corn Fritters are the perfect breakfast dish. If someone in your family prefers a sweeter start to their day, these fritters are also great served with butter and real maple syrup.
Serves 4.

PEAMEAL BACON
1 Tbsp (15 mL) vegetable oil
8 slices peameal bacon

FRITTERS
2 large eggs, separated
½ tsp (2 mL) fine sea salt
3 Tbsp (45 mL) all-purpose flour
1 cup (250 mL) fresh sweet corn kernels
¼ cup (60 mL) finely chopped fresh flat-leaf parsley
¼ cup (60 mL) vegetable oil (approx)

GARNISH
8 slices fresh beefsteak tomatoes
Finely chopped fresh flat-leaf parsley

Preheat the oven to 225°F (105°C).

PEAMEAL BACON
Place the oil in a large skillet set over medium heat. Once hot (see note), add the peameal bacon. Cook for 2 minutes on each side or until lightly browned and cooked through.

Transfer the cooked slices to a plate and cover with aluminum foil until needed.

Wipe down the surface of the skillet for use in making the fritters.

FRITTERS
Whisk together the egg whites and salt in the bowl of a stand mixer for 2 minutes or until stiff.

Whisk the egg yolks by hand in a medium-sized bowl for 2 minutes. Fold in the flour, corn, and parsley. Gently fold in the egg whites until just combined.

Add enough oil to coat the bottom of the skillet. Heat the oil over medium-high heat.

Add the batter to the hot oil in 2 Tbsp (30 mL) dollops. Do not overcrowd the pan. Gently flatten the fritters and fry for 2 minutes on each side or until golden brown. Place the completed fritters on a baking sheet and keep warm in the oven.

Add more oil to the pan, as needed, to fry remaining fritters.

ASSEMBLY
Set out 4 plates.

Place 2 corn fritters on each plate and top each with a slice of peameal bacon, a slice of tomato, and a sprinkling of parsley.

▶ True Canadian bacon, known as "peameal bacon," is made from boneless pork loin. Tender and unsmoked, peameal bacon is cured in a sweet pickle brine and rolled in a traditional golden cornmeal coating.

▶ To determine when oil is hot enough for frying, simply sprinkle a few drops of water over the pan. If the water sizzles on impact, the oil is ready.

garden vegetable frittata

A frittata is basically a no-fuss, no-work omelette. The flavours in this recipe are garden- and Greek-inspired. Serves 4.

2 Tbsp (30 mL) extra virgin olive oil

1 cup (250 mL) loosely packed fresh
  baby spinach

½ cup (125 mL) quartered fresh
  cherry tomatoes

½ cup (125 mL) finely chopped
  green onions

1 Tbsp (15 mL) finely chopped
  fresh oregano

6 large eggs

½ cup (125 mL) milk

¼ tsp (1 mL) fine sea salt

¼ tsp (1 mL) freshly ground black
  pepper

½ cup (125 mL) crumbled feta
  cheese

Preheat the oven to 375°F (190°C).

Heat the oil in a 9-inch (23 cm) skillet set over medium-high heat. Add the spinach, tomatoes, green onions, and oregano. Cook for 2 minutes, stirring often.

Whisk together the eggs, milk, salt, and pepper in a medium-sized bowl. Add the mixture to the skillet. Sprinkle with feta cheese.

Bake for 10 minutes or until the eggs are almost set. Remove the pan from the oven and cut into wedges.

Serve warm.

▶ When recipes call for a skillet, we suggest using a pan with a heavy bottom. We find that a well-seasoned cast iron skillet is best in almost all situations (see note on page 176).

oatmeal breakfast cookies

The oatmeal cookie category at the Harrow Fair is tough to win. Only hours after your family has assured you that yours are the best they've ever tasted, your cookies are disqualified for something crazy, like dark bottoms. Where is the justice in that? We changed strategies and enhanced the traditional oatmeal cookie with our favourite granola ingredients. Makes 24 cookies.

1 cup (250 mL) raisins

1 cup (250 mL) chopped dried apricots

½ cup (125 mL) genuine, pure maple syrup

1½ cups (375 mL) all-purpose flour

1 tsp (5 mL) baking powder

1 tsp (5 mL) ground cinnamon

1 tsp (5 mL) fine sea salt

1 cup (250 mL) unsalted butter, softened

½ cup (125 mL) firmly packed golden brown sugar

2 large eggs

2 tsp (10 mL) pure vanilla extract

3 cups (750 mL) old-fashioned rolled oats

½ cup (125 mL) chopped walnuts

¼ cup (60 mL) sunflower seeds

Position a rack in the centre of the oven. Preheat the oven to 350°F (180°C). Line a large baking sheet with parchment paper.

Mix together the raisins, apricots, and maple syrup in a small saucepan set over medium heat. Simmer for 5 minutes and set aside to cool.

Sift together the flour, baking powder, cinnamon, and salt in a medium-sized bowl.

In the bowl of a stand mixer fitted with the paddle attachment, cream together the butter and sugar until light and fluffy.

Beat in the eggs, one at a time, with the mixer on low speed. Beat in the vanilla. Add the dry ingredients to the batter, mixing on low speed until just combined. Add the raisin mixture, oats, walnuts, and sunflower seeds into the batter, mixing until just combined.

Place ¼-cup (60 mL) balls of dough (about the size of golf balls) on the baking sheet. Flatten dough balls to form 3-inch (8 cm) cookies.

Bake for 15 minutes or until golden brown. Remove the sheet to a rack and let stand for 1 minute. Transfer the cookies to racks to cool.

Serve warm.

STORAGE The cookies can be stored in an airtight container for up to 1 week.

summer fruit salad

We love serving this fruit salad at summer brunches. But instead of the typical jumble of colours, we go for a monochromatic look. The results are stunning. Serves 4.

8 cups (2 L) prepared fresh fruit
   (washed, peeled, and chopped in
   bite-sized pieces, as necessary)
¼ cup (60 mL) honey
¼ cup (60 mL) fresh lime juice
¼ cup (60 mL) finely chopped
   fresh mint

Place the prepared fruit in a large bowl.

Mix together the honey and lime juice in a small saucepan set over low heat. Stir until just melted, then add the chopped mint.

Pour the syrup over the fruit and gently toss.

Serve chilled.

monochromatic palettes

RED Watermelon + strawberries + black cherries + red raspberries

ORANGE Cantaloupe + peaches + nectarines + golden raspberries

PURPLE Purple plums + blueberries + blackberries + black raspberries

GREEN Honeydew melon + shiro plums + pears + green grapes

▷ Dresser's Purest Honey sells two types of honey at the Harrow Fair. Their wildflower honey is collected in the spring and summer from bees that have been pollinating a variety of local wildflowers. Their white honey is made mostly from bees that have been pollinating clover.

At the Harrow Fair, the Dressers also display a fascinating beehive for all to observe.

banana muffins

This has been our favourite muffin recipe for almost 20 years. Makes 12 muffins.

2 cups (500 mL) all-purpose flour

2½ tsp (12 mL) baking powder

½ tsp (2 mL) fine sea salt

½ cup (125 mL) unsalted butter, softened

1 cup (250 mL) + 1 Tbsp (15 mL) granulated sugar

2 large eggs

1 tsp (5 mL) pure vanilla extract

1½ cups (375 mL) mashed bananas

¼ cup (60 mL) milk

Preheat the oven to 375°F (190°C). Line a standard 12-muffin pan with paper muffin cups.

Sift together the flour, baking powder, and salt in a medium bowl.

In the bowl of a stand mixer fitted with the paddle attachment, cream together the butter and 1 cup (250 mL) sugar until light and fluffy.

Beat in the eggs, one at a time, with the mixer on low speed. Beat in the vanilla.

Combine the mashed bananas and milk in a small bowl.

With the mixer on low speed, add the flour mixture to the egg mixture in 3 parts, alternating with half the banana mixture (begin and end with the flour mixture). Mix until just combined.

Spoon the batter into the muffin cups. Sprinkle the muffin tops with the 1 Tbsp (15 mL) of sugar.

Bake for 25 minutes or until golden brown and a toothpick inserted into the centre of a muffin comes out clean.

Cool muffins for 10 minutes before removing from the pan.

STORAGE These muffins are at their best the day they are made.

▶ The batter for these muffins can easily be made into a cake. Simply butter an 8- × 8-inch (20 × 20 cm) pan and proceed with the instructions. Bake the cake for 40 minutes or until golden brown and a toothpick inserted into the centre of the cake comes out clean.

raspberry & lemon muffins

These are our go-to morning muffins when we have summer house guests. They're a cinch to make and turn out perfectly every time. Makes 12 muffins.

2 cups (500 mL) all-purpose flour
2½ tsp (12 mL) baking powder
½ tsp (2 mL) fine sea salt
½ cup (125 mL) unsalted butter, softened
1 cup (250 mL) granulated sugar
2 large eggs
1 Tbsp (15 mL) lemon zest
¾ cup (185 mL) milk
¼ cup (60 mL) fresh lemon juice
1½ cups (375 mL) fresh raspberries

Preheat the oven to 375°F (190°C). Line a standard 12-muffin pan with paper muffin cups.

Sift together the flour, baking powder, and salt in a large bowl.

In the bowl of a stand mixer fitted with the paddle attachment, cream together the butter and sugar until light and fluffy.

Beat in the eggs, one at a time, with the mixer on low speed. Beat in the lemon zest.

Combine the milk and lemon juice in a small bowl.

To the egg mixture, add the flour mixture alternately with the milk and lemon juice mixture (begin and end with the flour mixture). Mix until just combined. By hand, fold the raspberries into the batter until just combined.

Spoon the batter into the muffin cups.

Bake for 30 minutes or until golden brown and a toothpick inserted into the centre of the muffin comes out clean.

Cool for 10 minutes before serving.

STORAGE These muffins are at their best the day they are made.

▶ Feel free to substitute raspberries with other in-season berries, like blueberries and blackberries.

blueberry sour cream coffee cake

Klassen Blueberries is located in Oxley, a tiny hamlet just south of Harrow. Klassen's is the largest blueberry farm in our area and offers both pick-your-own and ready-picked berries. We love using their blueberries in this special coffee cake. Serves 8.

FILLING

1 cup (250 mL) firmly packed
    brown sugar
2 tsp (10 mL) ground cinnamon
¼ tsp (1 mL) fine sea salt
½ cup (125 mL) finely chopped
    toasted walnuts (see note on
    page 222)

BATTER

2 cups + 2 tsp (500 mL + 10 mL)
    all-purpose flour, divided
1 tsp (5 mL) baking powder
1 tsp (5 mL) baking soda
½ tsp (2 mL) fine sea salt
¾ cup (185 mL) unsalted butter,
    softened
1 cup (250 mL) granulated sugar
2 large eggs
1 tsp (5 mL) pure vanilla extract
1½ cups (375 mL) sour cream
1½ cups (375 mL) fresh blueberries

Preheat the oven to 350°F (180°C). Butter and flour a 10-inch (25 cm) tube pan.

FILLING

Mix together the sugar, cinnamon, salt, and walnuts in a medium-sized bowl. Set aside until needed.

BATTER

Sift together the 2 cups (500 mL) flour, baking powder, baking soda, and salt in a medium-sized bowl.

Cream the butter and sugar together in the bowl of a stand mixer. Beat in the eggs one at a time. Add the vanilla.

Add the dry ingredients to the wet ingredients, alternating with the sour cream (begin and end with the dry ingredients). Beat just until smooth.

Toss the blueberries with the 2 tsp (10 mL) flour and fold into the cake batter.

ASSEMBLY

Pour half the batter into the prepared tube pan. Sprinkle half the filling over the batter. Pour the remaining batter evenly around the pan. Sprinkle the remaining filling.

Bake for 50 minutes or until a toothpick inserted into the centre of the cake comes out clean.

Cool the cake in the pan for 15 minutes before inverting onto a large serving plate.

Cool to room temperature before serving.

▸ Mark your calendar: Essex County's blueberry season typically runs from mid-July until the beginning of September.

During blueberry season Klassen's is open 7 days a week. The farm is located along County Road 50 between Kingsville and Colchester. Just look for the big red barn.

Klassen's concession stand offers many homemade blueberry treats, including pies, tarts, and milkshakes.

▸ While fresh blueberries are ideal in this recipe, frozen blueberries work just as well. They can be added to the batter without thawing. However, the cake can take up to 15 minutes longer to bake.

currant & maple scones

These scones are the perfect breakfast pastry—flaky, moist, sweet, and decadent. They're also the perfect accompaniment to that first cup of morning coffee. Makes 12 scones.

2¼ cups (560 mL) all-purpose flour

1 cup (250 mL) whole wheat flour

¾ cup (185 mL) old-fashioned rolled oats

¼ cup + 1 Tbsp (60 mL + 15 mL) granulated sugar, divided

1½ Tbsp (22.5 mL) baking powder

1½ tsp (7 mL) fine sea salt

1½ cups (375 mL) cold unsalted butter, cubed

½ cup (125 mL) buttermilk (see note)

¼ cup (60 mL) pure maple syrup

3 large eggs

1 tsp (5 mL) pure vanilla extract

½ cup (125 mL) dried currants

1 large egg

1 Tbsp (15 mL) water

Preheat the oven to 400°F (200°C). Line a baking sheet with parchment paper.

Combine the flours, oats, the ¼ cup (60 mL) of sugar, baking powder, and salt in a large bowl. Incorporate the butter with your fingers or a pastry cutter until the largest pieces are the size of peas.

Stir together the buttermilk, maple syrup, eggs, and vanilla in a small bowl.

Pour the wet ingredients into the flour mixture, mixing until just combined. (The dough will be slightly sticky and tiny pieces of butter will be visible.) Stir in the currants until just combined.

Roll out the dough on a well-floured surface and shape it into a 10-inch (25 cm) circle. Cut the circle into 12 wedges. Transfer the scones to the baking sheet.

Mix together the egg and water. Brush the tops of the scones with the egg wash and sprinkle with the remaining 1 Tbsp (15 mL) of sugar.

Bake for 10 minutes. Rotate the baking sheet and bake for another 10 minutes.

Serve warm.

STORAGE Store scones in an airtight container for up to 2 days.

▶ Buttermilk is a low-fat milk that has had a culture added to it. If you can't find buttermilk in your grocery store, simply add ½ tsp (2 mL) white vinegar or lemon juice to ½ cup (125 mL) milk and stir. Let it stand for 5 minutes before using.

▶ For a more pronounced maple flavour, use Amber or Medium grades of maple syrup.

▶ The dough for these scones can be made ahead of time and then stored covered in the refrigerator for up to 2 days. Remove the dough from the refrigerator 30 minutes before baking.

pear cinnamon twists

We've been making these delicious breakfast treats for our family and neighbours in Harrow for years. Don't be intimidated by the lengthy directions—the twists are much easier to make than they might seem. Your mixer's dough hook provides the elbow grease. Makes 24 twists.

FILLING

1½ cups (375 mL) granulated sugar

2½ tsp (12 mL) ground cinnamon

½ tsp (2 mL) fine sea salt

2 cups (500 mL) peeled, cored, and chopped fresh pears (see second note)

1½ cups (375 mL) chopped toasted walnuts (see note on page 222)

DOUGH

⅓ cup + ¼ cup (80 mL + 60 mL) unsalted butter, divided

4½–5½ cups (1.125–1.375 L) all-purpose flour, divided

1½ tsp fine sea salt

2 packages/4½ tsp (22 mL) active dry yeast

1 cup (250 mL) milk

½ cup (125 mL) water

¼ cup (60 mL) honey

2 large eggs

1 cup (250 mL) raisins

THE
HARROW
FAIR

1st

FILLING

Combine the sugar, cinnamon, salt, pears, and walnuts in a medium-sized bowl.

DOUGH

Melt the ⅓ cup (80 mL) butter in a saucepan set over medium heat. Brush two 8- × 8-inch (20 × 20 cm) pans with half the melted butter. Set the remaining melted butter aside for use in a later step.

Place 2 cups (500 mL) of the flour, and the salt and yeast, in the bowl of a stand mixer fitted with the paddle attachment. Mix well.

Heat the ¼ cup (60 mL) butter, the milk, water, and honey in a saucepan until bubbles form around the edges of the pan.

Add the warm liquid and eggs to the dry ingredients in the mixing bowl. Mix on low speed until combined, then beat on medium speed for 3 minutes.

Add 2½ cups (625 mL) of the flour and the raisins, mixing until just combined.

Remove the paddle attachment and replace with a dough hook. (If you aren't using a dough hook, the dough can be kneaded by hand for 10 minutes on a well-floured surface.) Knead the dough on low speed for 10 minutes to form a stiff, barely sticky dough, scraping down the sides and hook as needed. Up to 1 cup (250 mL) of extra flour may be required.

Remove the dough from the hook and place it in the bottom of a greased mixing bowl. Cover the dough loosely with plastic wrap and a cloth towel, and let it sit at room temperature for 20 minutes.

Punch down the risen dough and divide it into 2 pieces. Roll 1 piece into a 12- × 12-inch (30 × 30 cm) square.

Brush the top of the dough with the remaining melted butter from the first step. Sprinkle 1 cup (250 mL) filling down the centre third (4 inches/10 cm) of the dough. Fold the left third (4 inches/10 cm) of the dough over the filling. Sprinkle this new layer with an additional 1 cup (250 mL) of filling. Fold the remaining right third of dough over this second layer of filling.

Cut the entire pastry crosswise into 12 even strips. Hold each strip at the top and bottom and twist in opposite directions 3 times. Transfer the completed twists to the baking pans, fitting them snugly into the pans. Repeat this entire procedure with the remaining half of the dough.

Cover the pans loosely with plastic wrap. Refrigerate for at least 2 hours and up to 24 hours.

Preheat the oven to 375°F (190°C). Uncover the twists and let them sit at room temperature for 10 minutes.

Bake for 30 minutes or until the twists are golden brown and sound hollow when tapped. If the twists are browning too quickly, cover them loosely with aluminum foil.

Remove the baked twists from the pans quickly by inverting them onto large serving plates.

Enjoy warm.

▶ In high school, Lori spent her summers working at Balsillie Fruit Farm. Doug and Leslie Balsillie's beautiful orchards are located along County Road 50, which follows the shore of Lake Erie between Kingsville and Harrow.

Among the many fruits Doug and Leslie grow, there are nine cultivars of pears. These are available from their roadside Fruit Wagon from August through October. Our favourite eating pears are Flemish Beauties—worth seeking out for their great texture and flavour.

▶ Bosc pears are great for this recipe because they retain their firm texture when baked in the twists.

peachy french toast

French toast always makes for a great breakfast, but when it's served with warm peaches it's elevated to a special treat. While any bread will work, try making it with a rich, egg-based bread, like brioche or Portuguese sweet bread. Serves 4.

FRENCH TOAST

3 large eggs
½ cup (125 mL) milk
½ cup (125 mL) whipping cream
½ tsp (2 mL) fine sea salt
8 bread slices
5 Tbsp (75 mL) unsalted butter
    (approx)

PEACHES

½ cup (125 mL) unsalted butter
3 cups (750 mL) peeled, pitted, and
    sliced fresh peaches
½ cup (125 mL) firmly packed
    brown sugar
½ tsp (2 mL) ground cinnamon

THE
HARROW
FAIR

authors'
FAVE

FRENCH TOAST

Preheat the oven to 250°F (120°C).

Whisk together the eggs, milk, whipping cream, and salt in a shallow bowl. Dip 2 bread slices into the egg mixture until well coated.

Heat 2 Tbsp (30 mL) of butter in a large skillet set over medium heat. When the butter is sizzling, cook the slices for 2 minutes on each side or until browned.

Transfer the completed slices to a baking sheet and keep warm in the oven.

Repeat the steps, using more butter in the skillet, as necessary, until the remaining slices are cooked.

PEACHES

Melt the butter in a saucepan set over medium-high heat. Add the peaches and cook for 2 minutes or until they are warm and softened.

Stir in the brown sugar and cinnamon. Cook until the sugar has dissolved and the mixture is bubbling.

ASSEMBLY

Set out 4 plates. Place 2 pieces of french toast on each plate, then cover with warm peaches. Serve warm.

zucchini bread

This fabulous, moist zucchini bread was a ribbon winner for Lisa Renaud. Lisa and her family, who live in Amherstburg, have been attending the Harrow Fair for almost two decades. Makes 2 loaves.

3 cups (750 mL) all-purpose flour
1 tsp (5 mL) fine sea salt
1 tsp (5 mL) baking powder
1 tsp (5 mL) baking soda
3 tsp (15 mL) ground cinnamon
3 large eggs
1 cup (250 mL) vegetable oil
2¼ cups (560 mL) granulated sugar
3 tsp (15 mL) pure vanilla extract
2 cups (500 mL) grated zucchini
1 cup (250 mL) chopped toasted
    walnuts (see note on page 222)

THE
HARROW
FAIR

1st

Preheat the oven to 325°F (160°C). Grease and flour two 8- × 4-inch (1.5 L) loaf pans.

Stir together the flour, salt, baking powder, baking soda, and cinnamon in a medium-sized bowl. In a large bowl, beat together the eggs, oil, sugar, and vanilla.

Add the flour mixture to the egg mixture and beat until just combined. Add the zucchini and nuts to the batter, stirring until just combined.

Pour the batter into the prepared pans. Bake for 45 minutes or until a toothpick inserted into the centre of a loaf comes out clean.

Set the pans on a baking rack to cool. Once cool, remove the zucchini bread from the pans.

Slice and serve.

STORAGE The loaves will keep for 5 days at room temperature if covered in plastic wrap.

Zucchini bread also freezes brilliantly. Simply cover the loaves in plastic wrap, place them in a resealable plastic bag, and store them in the freezer. Allow the loaves to defrost gradually at room temperature, still wrapped, for several hours prior to serving.

▶ Zucchini bread can easily be transformed into zucchini muffins. Follow the recipe steps, then spoon the batter into muffin cups, filling them at least three-quarters full. Bake at 350°F (180°C) for 35 minutes or until golden brown and a toothpick inserted into the centre of a muffin comes out clean. Makes 2 dozen.

apple & oatmeal pancakes

We have tried countless pancake recipes over the years, but this is the one we return to again and again. When a stack of these is drizzled with warm maple syrup, no one can resist them. Serves 4.

1¼ cups (310 mL) old-fashioned
    rolled oats
1 cup (250 mL) plain yogurt
1 cup (250 mL) milk
1 Tbsp (15 mL) honey
½ cup (125 mL) all-purpose flour
1 tsp (5 mL) baking soda
½ tsp (2 mL) fine sea salt
2 large eggs, beaten
1 cup (250 mL) grated apple
2 Tbsp (30 mL) unsalted butter
    (approx)
2 Tbsp (30 mL) vegetable oil
    (approx)
Pure maple syrup

Stir together the rolled oats, yogurt, milk, and honey in a large bowl. Stir in the flour, baking soda, and salt.

Mix in the beaten eggs, until just combined. Fold in the grated apples, until just combined.

Heat approximately 1 Tbsp (15 mL) of butter and 1 Tbsp (15 mL) of oil in a large skillet over medium heat. When the butter and oil start to sizzle, spoon ¼-cup (60 mL) dollops of batter onto the hot skillet. Do not overcrowd.

Cook for 3 minutes or until the bottoms begin to brown and the bubbles on top begin to pop. Flip and cook for 2 minutes or until the second side is browned.

Repeat the steps, using more butter and oil in the skillet as necessary, until no batter remains.

Serve hot with an abundance of pure maple syrup.

▶ One of the most intensively farmed regions in the country, Essex County is less than 4 percent forested. The trees that remain are part of what was once a vast deciduous forest enclosed by lakes Ontario, Erie, and Huron.

Native species, most of which reached their northern growth limit in the region, included varieties of chestnut, tulip tree, hickory, oak, black walnut, sycamore, butternut, beech, magnolia, papaw, mulberry, sassafras, and both silver and red maple.

There are still several maple syrup producers in our area. They tap the trees near the end of winter, collect the sap, and then boil it down to a syrup.

HAPPY HOURS

bloody good caesars
   made with homemade
   tomato juice

picnic table iced tea

lemon shake-ups

watermelon martinis

nectarine daiquiris

rhubarb punch

pelee island sangria

local whisky sours

nuts for happy hour(s)

cheddar loonies

bloody good caesars

If Canada had a national cocktail this would be it. The typical Bloody Caesar is served on the rocks in a glass rimmed with celery salt and garnished with a stalk of celery and a wedge of lime. For a fun twist, set up a Bloody Good Caesar Bar where everyone can create their own version. Serves 4.

4 cups (1 L) homemade tomato juice
1 cup (250 mL) clam juice
¼ cup (60 mL) Worcestershire sauce
2 Tbsp (30 mL) fresh lime juice
1 tsp (5 mL) Tabasco sauce
¼ cup (60 mL) celery salt (approx)
Lime wedge for moistening rim
8 fl oz (250 mL) vodka (approx)

Place the tomato juice, clam juice, Worcestershire sauce, lime juice, and Tabasco sauce in a serving pitcher and stir. Chill for at least 1 hour (and up to 24 hours) prior to serving.

ASSEMBLY

Select glasses for the Caesars. (We love serving them in glass canning jars.)

Spread the celery salt out on a small plate. Moisten the rim of each glass with a lime wedge, then twist the rim into the celery salt. Shake off any excess salt and set the glasses upright. Fill each glass with ice cubes.

Pour 1 to 2 fl oz (30 to 60 mL) of vodka per glass. (The amount of vodka used depends on personal preference and/or the level of hangover in need of a remedy.) Fill the glasses with the Caesar mix.

Garnish with ingredients from the Bloody Good Caesar Bar.

homemade tomato juice

Using homemade tomato juice in your Caesars (versus the store-bought stuff) is the difference between floating on the lake in a leaky rowboat and cruising around on a luxury yacht. Making the juice is surprisingly easy. Just be sure to use ripe tomatoes. Makes 4 cups (1 L).

8 cups (2 L) chopped fresh tomatoes
2 cups (500 mL) chopped celery, with stalks and leaves
1 cup (250 mL) chopped yellow onion
1 Tbsp (15 mL) granulated sugar
2 tsp (10 mL) fine sea salt
½ tsp (2 mL) freshly ground black pepper

Combine the ingredients in a large stockpot. Bring the contents to a boil over medium-high heat, then reduce the heat to low, stirring occasionally. Simmer for 35 minutes or until the vegetables are tender.

Purée the mixture in a food processor or blender. Strain the juice through a sieve into a serving pitcher. Chill until ready to use in the Bloody Good Caesars recipe.

STORAGE The juice can be stored in an airtight container in the refrigerator for up to 3 days.

bloody good caesar bar

Prepared horseradish
Celery stalks
Dill pickles (page 26)
Stuffed manzanillo olives
Pickled asparagus (page 29)
Pickled green beans
Lime wedges

POLAR ICE VODKA For really local Caesars, try making them with Polar Ice vodka (www.polarice.ca). Polar Ice is produced in the nearby city of Windsor, Ontario, located along the Detroit River, just 40 kilometres (23 miles) north of Harrow. Made from 100 percent Canadian wheat, Polar Ice vodka is quadruple distilled.

picnic table iced tea

There's nothing like a glass of iced tea on a hot summer's day. For a unique and refreshing twist, try making it with basil leaves. Serves 4.

2 orange pekoe tea bags
6 large fresh basil leaves
½ lemon, sliced
8 cups (2 L) boiling water
¼ cup (60 mL) granulated sugar
(optional)

Place the tea bags, basil leaves, and lemon slices in a heatproof glass pitcher. Pour in the boiling water. Stir in the sugar, if using.

Set the pitcher out on a picnic table and let steep for 10 minutes. Remove the tea bags.

Pour tea over ice cubes in large glasses.

▶ Since 1894, Canada's favourite national brand of tea has been Red Rose.

lemon shake-ups

Lemon Shake-ups are the quintessential refreshing drink of country fairs. Fortunately, they're easy to re-create at home. Just squeeze and shake 'em up. Serves 4.

1 cup (250 mL) fresh lemon juice
  (see note)
4 cups (1 L) crushed ice
2 cups (500 mL) cold water
½ cup (125 mL) berry sugar
1 lemon, cut into wedges

Set out 4 large glasses, at least 12 fl oz (375 mL) in size.

For each drink, fill a metal cocktail shaker with ¼ cup (60 mL) lemon juice, 1 cup (250 mL) crushed ice, ½ cup (125 mL) cold water, and 2 Tbsp (30 mL) berry sugar.

Cover the shaker with its lid or a glass. Shake vigorously for 30 seconds. Pour the beverage into a glass. Repeat for the remaining glasses.

Garnish each glass with a wedge of lemon.

▸ To extract lemon juice, start with lemons at room temperature. Roll the lemons underneath your palms on a countertop for a few seconds; this will make them much easier to juice. Juice the lemons. Strain the juice to eliminate the seeds and pulp.

▸ For an adult-friendly version of Lemon Shake-ups, add 1 to 2 fl oz (30 to 60 mL) of vodka per glass.

▸ Lime juice can be used to make Lime Shake-ups. Simply substitute lime juice for the lemon juice and enjoy.

watermelon martinis

When we asked our friend and summertime neighbour Kristin Merz to test drink recipes for the cookbook, she eagerly agreed to help. On one occasion she left a conversation with her husband mid-sentence when we yelled (from four doors down) that it was time to try another round. She's a true friend. To us . . . and to a good cocktail.

Makes 4 generous martinis.

4 cups (1 L) seeded and chopped
    fresh watermelon
1 cup (250 mL) vodka
¼ cup (60 mL) Cointreau or triple sec
¼ cup (60 mL) fresh lime juice
4 ice cubes
1 Tbsp (15 mL) berry sugar
4 small watermelon wedges

Place the watermelon chunks, vodka, Cointreau, and 4 glasses in the freezer for at least 1 hour before preparing the martinis.

Blend the watermelon, vodka, Cointreau, lime juice, and ice cubes in a blender. Taste and add the berry sugar, if desired. Strain and divide into the 4 chilled glasses and garnish each with a small wedge of watermelon.

Serve immediately.

▶ WATERMELON KIDTINIS Blend 4 cups (1 L) watermelon chunks and ¼ cup (60 mL) fresh lime juice with 1 Tbsp (15 mL) berry sugar. Serve over ice with straws and garnish with a small wedge of watermelon. (Serves 4.)

SONGS FOR SUMMER SIPPING

On a hot summer afternoon, this is what we'd play to get everybody smiling ... Well, this and a few rounds of daiquiris wouldn't hurt either.

We're Here for a Good Time — TROOPER • *Coconut* — HARRY NILSSON • *Good Vibrations* — THE BEACH BOYS • *In the Summertime* — MUNGO JERRY • *Under the Boardwalk* — THE DRIFTERS • *All Summer Long* — KID ROCK • *Keep It Comin' Love* — KC AND THE SUNSHINE BAND • *Shout* — THE ISLEY BROTHERS • *Jungle Love* — STEVE MILLER • *Great Lakes Song* — PAT DAILEY • *(Shake, Shake, Shake) Shake Your Booty* — KC AND THE SUNSHINE BAND • *Saturday in the Park* — CHICAGO • *Working for the Weekend* — LOVERBOY • *Feelin' Alright* — JOE COCKER • *Fun, Fun, Fun* — THE BEACH BOYS • *Day-O (The Banana Boat Song)* — HARRY BELAFONTE • *Summer Nights* — OLIVIA NEWTON-JOHN & JOHN TRAVOLTA • *Dancing in the Moonlight* — KING HARVEST • *Sundown* — GORDON LIGHTFOOT

nectarine daiquiris

This is our family's favourite summertime drink. For the adults, there's rum. For the kids, there's no rum . . . but there are cute paper umbrellas and straws. Serves 4.

6 cups (1.5 L) sliced fresh nectarines
¼ cup (60 mL) berry sugar
½ cup (125 mL) fresh lime juice
4 cups (1 L) ice cubes
¾ cup (185 mL) white rum
1 lime, cut into wedges

Chill the glasses for at least 1 hour before preparing the daiquiris.

Purée the nectarines, sugar, lime juice, ice cubes, and rum in a blender. (There's no need to remove the skins from the nectarines used in this cocktail. They add pretty red flecks to the drink.) Add more sugar, if needed.

Divide into the 4 chilled glasses and garnish each with a wedge of lime.

Serve immediately.

rhubarb punch

This recipe is based on a version made by our aunt Karen Goslin. It's now the family-friendly drink of choice at our gatherings. We prefer it when it's made with club soda, but for a more traditional, sweeter punch, use ginger ale. Serves 16.

2 large oranges
8 cups (2 L) water
12 cups (3 L) chopped fresh rhubarb
2½ cups (625 mL) granulated sugar
8 cups (2 L) club soda, cold
Orange slices for garnish

Wash the 2 large oranges well. Using a vegetable peeler, peel the zest off of the oranges in wide strips.

Place the water, rhubarb, and strips of orange zest in a stockpot set over high heat. Boil the mixture for 10 minutes.

Strain the rhubarb and orange zest, reserving the liquid in a large punch bowl. Discard the pulp and zest. Stir the sugar into the hot liquid.

Store the concentrated punch in the refrigerator. Mix the concentrate with an equal part of club soda just prior to serving.

Serve over ice and garnish with orange slices.

STORAGE This punch can be made well in advance and frozen in containers. Simply defrost for a few hours in the refrigerator before use and add the club soda at the last minute.

▶ This recipe calls for fresh rhubarb, but frozen rhubarb works just as well.

pelee island sangria

Canada's very first commercial winery, Vin Villa, was established on Pelee Island in 1866. Today, the island is home to the highly regarded Pelee Island Winery. This sangria is a refreshing, fun way to enjoy one of the vintner's lovely dry white wines. Serves 8.

2 cups (500 mL) seedless green grapes
1 cup (250 mL) peeled, cored, and chopped apples
¼ cup (60 mL) fresh mint leaves, packed
½ cup (125 mL) berry sugar
2 Tbsp (30 mL) fresh lemon juice
Two 24 oz (750 mL) bottles Pelee Island Winery Sauvignon Blanc or Pinot Gris

Place the grapes, apples, mint, sugar, lemon juice, and 2 cups (500 mL) of the wine in a food processor. Process until smooth.

Pour the mixture into a large pitcher. Stir in the remaining wine. Cover and chill for at least 2 hours and up to 24 hours.

Serve over ice.

▶ PELEE ISLAND WINERY Pelee Island Winery (www.peleeisland .com) is the only winery in the VQA-designated appellation of Pelee Island. The vineyard's picturesque pavilion is a great place to sample recent vintages.

▶ PELEE ISLAND Located in the middle of Lake Erie, Pelee Island is the southernmost point in Canada. At 4,000 hectares (10,000 acres) it is also the largest island in Lake Erie.

The island has developed a reputation for appealing to wine connoisseurs, but boaters, cyclists, hikers, and nature enthusiasts can all enjoy the island's unspoiled beauty and rustic simplicity. It's a wonderful place for a day trip or weekend getaway. The island is easily accessible by ferry from Kingsville or Leamington.

THE WINERIES OF LAKE ERIE'S NORTH SHORE

In 2000, Lake Erie North Shore was deemed a Designated Viticultural Area by Canada's Vintners Quality Alliance (VQA). The area is, to completely understate it, suitable for grape growing:

- The appellation shares its latitude with the world-class wine regions of the Napa Valley, California; Tuscany, Italy; and Bordeaux, France.
- It has one of the longest growing seasons in the country.
- Its seasons are tempered by the presence of Lake Erie. In the summer the breezes from the lake cool the vineyards, and in the fall and winter, the lake helps keep the coldest temperatures at bay.

There are more than a dozen wineries in the Lake Erie North Shore appellation. Collectively, they're helping to establish the area as one of Canada's finest wine regions—they are producing some truly lovely wines. Standouts include several full-bodied red wines and a number of sweet, rich late-harvest wines.

Here are a few of our favourite producers:

COLCHESTER RIDGE ESTATE WINERY
www.colchesterridge.com
CREW's vineyard is surrounded by grapevines and lush green fields. Their reserve wines are all made from estate-grown grapes. Owner and winemaker Bernie Gorski's favourite wine is his rich, fruit-forward Cabernet Sauvignon.

COLIO ESTATE WINES
www.colio.com
Established in 1980, Colio is credited with reviving grape growing and wine production in Essex County. Colio Estate Vineyards (CEV) Reserve label is made from grapes grown entirely on Colio's local vineyards. The vintner has won a number of international awards for the fruity and floral CEV Vidal Icewine.

ERIE SHORE VINEYARD
www.erieshore.ca
The Hollingshead family's vineyard is located a stone's throw from Lake Erie. Their best selling wine is Summer Sun Cabernet, a citrusy, semi-sweet rosé. All Erie Shore Vineyard's wines are estate grown.

SANSON ESTATE WINERY
dsanson.mnsi.net
Sanson Estate Winery is a wine and food destination. Owner and winemaker Dennis Sanson produces a number of fine, critically acclaimed wines. Baco Noir is his personal favourite—and a favourite among his customers.

SPRUCEWOOD SHORES ESTATE WINERY
www.sprucewoodshores.com
Located right on the shores of Lake Erie, the Mitchell family's warm and inviting winery is arguably the prettiest in the region. Winemaker Tanya Mitchell crafts all her wines from grapes grown on the property. Their crisp, semi-sweet Riesling is one of their most popular wines.

VIEWPOINTE ESTATE WINERY
www.viewpointewinery.com
As its name suggests, Viewpointe Estate Winery possesses gorgeous views of the lake. The property's vines produce the grapes that go into Viewpointe's 100 percent estate-grown wines. Winemaker John Fancsy's personal favourite is Balance Pointe, a full-bodied and bold wine that's a blend of Cabernet and Merlot.

local whisky sours

We took a classic cocktail, the Whisky Sour, and made it local by adding fresh sour cherry juice. Serves 4.

1 cup (250 mL) Canadian Club whisky
1 cup (250 mL) fresh lemon juice
½ cup (125 mL) fresh sour cherry juice
¼ cup (60 mL) berry sugar
4 cups (1 L) crushed ice
Lemon wedges
Fresh sour cherries

Set out 4 large glasses, at least 12 fl oz (375 mL) in size.

For each drink, fill a metal cocktail shaker with ¼ cup (60 mL) whisky, ¼ cup (60 mL) lemon juice, 2 Tbsp (30 mL) sour cherry juice, 1 Tbsp (15 mL) berry sugar, and 1 cup (250 mL) crushed ice.

Cover the shaker with its lid or a glass. Shake vigorously for 30 seconds. Pour the beverage into a glass. Repeat for the remaining glasses.

Garnish each glass with a wedge of lemon and fresh sour cherries.

Serve immediately.

▶ CANADIAN CLUB In 1858, American distiller Hiram Walker came to Canada and established operations on the east side of Windsor, Ontario. By the turn of the century, Walker's Canadian Club whisky and his model community, Walkerville, were world-famous. Canadian Club even received the royal warrant (and patronage) of Queen Victoria.

Known for being "lighter than scotch, smoother than bourbon," Canadian Club (www.canadianclubwhisky.com) is a well-balanced whisky that hints of butterscotch, vanilla, and orange rind.

Canadian Club was particularly popular during Prohibition, which lasted from 1920 to 1933 in the United States. One of the distillery's most famous clients was Chicago gangster Al Capone. (He also liked Walker's beer (see note on page 114).)

To this day, area residents have stories about great-grandparents who were smugglers. In winter, some even drove cases of whisky from Walkerville across the frozen Detroit River to awaiting (thirsty) bootleggers.

nuts for happy hour(s)

No one hosts happy hour(s) as well as the Jenner family, our next-door neighbours for more than 30 years. This fun-loving family draws friends and neighbours to their beach cottage every summer afternoon. (Anyone with a dry mouth is welcome. Sandy dogs included!) These addictive little nuts are just the kind of thing the Jenners would serve.
Makes 4 cups (1 L).

4 cups (1 L) raw, unsalted mixed nuts
    (pecans, almonds, peanuts, and
    cashews)
¼ cup (60 mL) pure maple syrup
2 tsp (10 mL) chopped fresh rosemary
1 tsp (5 mL) chili powder
1 tsp (5 mL) fine sea salt

Preheat the oven to 375°F (190°C). Line a large baking sheet with parchment paper.

Spread the nuts out on the baking sheet and toast for 8 to 10 minutes, stirring once, until they are darker in colour and their nutty fragrance is released. Setting a timer will help make sure you don't burn the nuts.

Mix together the toasted nuts, maple syrup, rosemary, and chili powder in a large bowl.

Spread the nut mixture out on the baking sheet and bake for 15 minutes or until the syrup begins to bubble.

Sprinkle with the salt. Leave the nuts on the tray to cool to room temperature.

STORAGE These nuts will keep for up to 2 weeks in an airtight container at room temperature.

cheddar loonies

These savoury shortbread crackers are made to be the same size as Canada's $1 "loonie" coin. We're sure you'll agree that the taste is worth much more. Makes 4 dozen.

2½ cups (625 mL) all-purpose flour
1½ tsp (7 mL) fine sea salt
⅛ tsp (0.5 mL) cayenne pepper
1 cup (250 mL) unsalted butter, softened
2 cups (500 mL) shredded sharp Canadian cheddar cheese
2 tsp (10 mL) finely chopped fresh thyme

Sift together the flour, salt, and cayenne pepper in a medium-sized bowl. Cream the butter for 2 minutes in the bowl of a stand mixer. Mix in the shredded cheese and thyme.

Add the dry ingredients to the butter mixture. Mix on low speed until the dough comes together.

Turn the dough out onto a floured surface and knead gently. Form the dough into a disc, then divide in half. Roll each half into a cylinder slightly larger than 1 inch (2.5 cm) in diameter. (Loonies are 2.65 cm, or a little less than 1¹⁄₁₆ inch, in diameter.) Wrap each cylinder in parchment paper.

Refrigerate for at least 1 hour and up to 24 hours.

Preheat the oven to 350°F (180°C). Line a large baking sheet with parchment paper.

Slice the dough into ¼-inch (6 mm) loonies. Bake for 20 minutes or until golden brown.

Cool the loonies on a baking rack.

Serve warm or at room temperature.

STORAGE Cylinders of the dough can be stored in the freezer for up to 3 months. Thaw for 1 hour on a countertop before slicing the dough.

The baked loonies can be stored in an airtight container for up to 1 week. (Do not store in a piggy bank.)

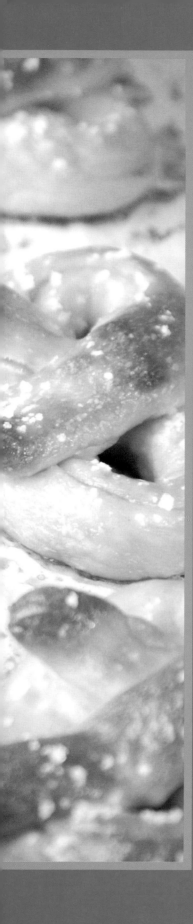

STARTERS

soft pretzels

Tired of having to wait until the weekend of the Harrow Fair to enjoy soft pretzels? Take matters into your own hands and whip up a batch. These will satisfy your cravings—at least for a little while. They are delicious with honey mustard sauce (next page). Makes 16 pretzels.

1½ cups (375 mL) water, heated to
    110°F (43°C)
1 Tbsp (15 mL) granulated sugar
2 tsp (10 mL) fine sea salt
1 Tbsp (15 mL) active dry yeast
4½ cups (1.125 L) all-purpose flour
2 Tbsp (30 mL) unsalted butter
1 Tbsp (15 mL) vegetable oil
½ cup (125 mL) baking soda
1 egg yolk
1 Tbsp (15 mL) water
¼ cup (60 mL) coarse kosher salt

Combine the warm water, sugar, and salt in the bowl of a stand mixer fitted with the dough hook attachment. Sprinkle the yeast on top. Let the mixture sit for 5 minutes, until it begins to foam.

Add the flour and butter. Mix on low speed until the dough starts to come together. Mix on medium for 5 minutes or until the dough is smooth and comes together into a ball.

Grease a large, clean bowl with oil. Place the dough into the bowl, turning it to ensure it is well coated. Cover the bowl with plastic wrap and let it sit in a warm spot for 1 hour or until the dough has doubled in size.

Preheat the oven to 425°F (220°C). Line a large baking sheet with parchment paper.

Bring a large saucepan of water to a boil. Add the baking soda.

While the water is heating, remove the dough from the bowl. Cut into 16 equal wedges. Roll each piece of dough into a 12-inch (30 cm) rope. Make a U shape with the rope. Cross the ends over each other and press together at the bottom of the U to form a pretzel shape. Transfer the pretzels to the baking sheet.

Add the pretzels, one at a time, to the boiling water for 30 seconds. Remove the pretzels from the water, and return them to the baking sheet.

Beat together the egg yolk and water. Brush each pretzel with the egg wash. Generously sprinkle each pretzel with the kosher salt.

Bake for 15 minutes or until the pretzels are dark golden brown and smell amazing.

Cool for 5 minutes on a rack.

Serve warm with honey mustard sauce.

STORAGE These pretzels are at their best the day they are made.

(honey mustard sauce recipe follows)

soft pretzels *(continued)*

honey mustard sauce

¼ cup (60 mL) yellow mustard
¼ cup (60 mL) grainy mustard
2 Tbsp (30 mL) honey

Combine the mustards and the honey. Taste and add more honey, if necessary.

▶ The Canadian Salt Company was founded in 1893 in Windsor, Ontario. The company has become Canada's largest salt manufacturer—involved in the recovery, processing, and marketing of more than 200 salt products. For our soft pretzels, we love Windsor's coarse kosher salt.

toasted crisps

Having a container of Toasted Crisps on hand means you'll always be ready for company.
They're a cinch to make and are the perfect partner for all sorts of dips and cheeses.

Serves 4.

1 large baguette
½ cup (125 mL) extra virgin olive oil
  (approx)
1 tsp (5 mL) fine sea salt

Preheat the oven to 350°F (180°C).

Cut the baguette into slices about ¼ inch (6 mm) thick. Brush each slice with olive oil and place on a baking sheet. Sprinkle with salt.

Bake for 10 minutes. Turn each slice over and bake for another 10 minutes or until golden and crispy.

Cool before serving.

STORAGE   Store in an airtight container for up to 1 week.

smoked trout dip

Smoked trout has a mild, smoky flavour that works really well with the dill and capers in this recipe. Spread generously on Toasted Crisps (page 79). This dip is very good the day it is made, but even better the next day. Serves 4.

1 cup (250 mL) cream cheese,
    softened
1 cup (250 mL) flaked smoked trout
¼ cup (60 mL) sliced green onions
2 Tbsp (30 mL) finely chopped
    fresh dill
2 Tbsp (30 mL) finely chopped
    capers
1 Tbsp (15 mL) fresh lemon juice
⅓ cup (80 mL) sour cream
½ tsp (2 mL) fine sea salt
¼ tsp (1 mL) freshly ground
    black pepper

Mix together the cream cheese and trout in a medium-sized bowl. Stir in the rest of the ingredients until thoroughly mixed. Serve chilled.

▶ Trout, which is native to the Great Lakes, is not fished commercially on Lake Erie. It's for anglers only.

THE
HARROW
FAIR

authors'
FAVE

three-onion dip

Made with yellow, red, and green onions, this is the ultimate homemade chip dip.

Serves 4.

¼ cup (60 mL) extra virgin olive oil

2 cups (500 mL) thinly sliced yellow onion

1 cup (250 mL) thinly sliced red onion

⅛ tsp (0.5 mL) cayenne pepper

1 tsp (5 mL) fine sea salt

½ tsp (2 mL) freshly ground black pepper

¾ cup (185 mL) sour cream

¾ cup (185 mL) mayonnaise (page 85)

½ cup (125 mL) cream cheese, softened

½ cup (125 mL) thinly sliced green onions

Heat the olive oil in a large skillet set over medium-low heat. Add the yellow and red onions, cayenne pepper, salt, and pepper. Cook for 30 minutes, stirring frequently, or until the onions have caramelized.

Mix together the sour cream, mayonnaise, and cream cheese in a large bowl. Stir in the cooked mixture. Add the green onions.

Let the dip sit for at least 1 hour before serving with potato chips. Serve chilled or at room temperature.

STORAGE   The dip can be refrigerated for up to 5 days, until ready to serve.

tomato & goat cheese topping

Mouthwatering *is the best way to describe this starter.* Serves 4.

2 cups (500 mL) cored, seeded, and
    diced fresh tomatoes
12 kalamata olives, chopped
1 garlic clove, minced
2 anchovy fillets, finely chopped
¼ cup (60 mL) finely chopped
    shallots
2 Tbsp (30 mL) finely chopped
    fresh basil
1½ Tbsp (22 mL) fresh lemon juice
3 Tbsp (45 mL) extra virgin olive oil
½ tsp (2 mL) fine sea salt
¼ tsp (1 mL) freshly ground black
    pepper
¼ lb (125 g) goat cheese, softened
Toasted Crisps (page 79)

Mix together the tomatoes, olives, garlic, anchovies, shallots, basil, lemon juice, olive oil, salt, and pepper in a medium-sized bowl. Refrigerate for at least 15 minutes or up to 24 hours.

Spread a generous amount of goat cheese on a Toasted Crisp, then top with a heaping spoonful of the tomato mixture.

devilish eggs

The inclusion of homemade mayo, fresh garden herbs, and fresh lemon juice takes this classic recipe in a devilishly good direction. Makes 24.

12 large eggs
¾ cup (185 mL) mayonnaise
(facing page)
¼ tsp (1 mL) fine sea salt
¼ cup (60 mL) finely chopped fresh
chives
2 Tbsp (30 mL) finely chopped fresh
flat-leaf parsley
1 tsp (5 mL) fresh lemon juice
½ tsp (2 mL) smoked paprika
(approx)

Gently place the eggs in the bottom of a large pot. Cover the eggs by 1 inch (2.5 cm) with well-salted cold water. Bring to a boil, turn off the heat, and cover the pan with a lid. Let the eggs sit for 10 minutes before draining the water and refilling the pot with cold water. Let the eggs cool for an additional 20 minutes.

Carefully peel the eggs (see note below).

Cut the eggs in half, lengthwise. Place the egg whites on a serving plate.

Place the yolks in the bowl of a food processor. Add the mayonnaise, salt, chives, parsley, and lemon juice and blend until smooth.

Spoon the yolk mixture back into the egg whites. Sprinkle a tiny amount of smoked paprika on each devilish egg.

Serve chilled.

▶ PEELING HARD-BOILED EGGS Perfectly peeled eggs are important for making this appetizer look, well, appetizing. Surprisingly, the key to having eggs that peel easily is to use eggs that are at least a week old.

When the eggs have been cooked and cooled, drain off some of the water, leaving enough in the pan to just barely cover the eggs.

Shake the saucepan with the eggs and water in it, hard enough to break the shells on the eggs. (This is actually quite fun.) The water will get in between the shell and the eggs, making them easier to peel.

Drain off the rest of the water. Peel the eggs carefully.

mayonnaise

Homemade mayonnaise is infinitely better than store-bought versions, in both flavour and appearance. For a truly great mayonnaise, use the freshest eggs available. Makes 1 cup (250 mL).

1 large egg yolk
1½ tsp (7 mL) Dijon mustard
1½ tsp (7 mL) white wine vinegar
½ tsp (2 mL) fine sea salt
¼ tsp (1 mL) freshly ground black
　 pepper
1 cup (250 mL) vegetable oil

Mix together the egg yolk, mustard, vinegar, salt, and pepper in the bowl of a stand mixer fitted with the whisk attachment.

Pour ¼ cup (60 mL) of the oil in slow, steady drops with the mixer on medium.

Add the remaining oil, but at a slightly faster rate. Mix just until the oil is combined and the mayonnaise is the desired consistency.

STORAGE　The mayonnaise can be stored, covered, in the refrigerator for up to 1 week.

smoked whitefish & potato cakes

This easy but impressive appetizer features a fish native to Lake Erie. You can some-times find smoked whitefish at the Kingsville Fishermen's Company on the Kingsville dock, but if you're not in the neighbourhood, smoked trout or smoked salmon works just as well. Makes about 12 cakes.

POTATO CAKES

3 large Yukon Gold potatoes
1½ tsp (7 mL) fine sea salt
Vegetable oil, for frying

TOPPINGS

1 cup (250 mL) sour cream
⅓ lb (170 g) smoked whitefish
¼ cup (60 mL) chopped fresh chives

POTATO CAKES

Peel the potatoes, then shred them using the grater attachment on a food processor or a box grater with large holes. Sprinkle with salt, then toss.

Set a large skillet over medium-high heat. Add oil to the skillet until it is ½ inch (1 cm) in depth.

Add the potatoes to the hot oil in 2 Tbsp (30 mL) dollops. Do not overcrowd the pan. Gently flatten the cakes and fry for 2 to 3 minutes on each side, until golden brown.

Place fried cakes on a plate lined with paper towels to drain. Add more oil to the pan to fry remaining cakes, as needed.

ASSEMBLY

Place a small dollop of sour cream on each cake and top with a 1-inch (2.5 cm) piece of whitefish.

Garnish each cake with a bit of chopped chives.

Serve immediately.

▶ The cakes can be made in advance and re-warmed in a 300°F (150°C) oven for 5 minutes.

stuffed mushrooms

The recipe for these stuffed mushrooms was taught to us more than 20 years ago by our dear friend and summertime neighbour Evie Kozleski. They're so good and so easy.

Serves 4.

16 button mushrooms, 1½–2 inches (4–5 cm) in diameter
1 Tbsp (15 mL) unsalted butter
⅓ cup (80 mL) thinly sliced green onion
1 garlic clove, minced
1 cup (250 mL) cream cheese, softened
½ tsp (2 mL) fine sea salt
¼ tsp (1 mL) freshly ground black pepper

Preheat oven to 375°F (190°C).

Remove the mushroom stems completely and set aside. Gently brush any dirt from the mushrooms with a paper towel. (Do not wash the mushrooms as they will retain too much water.) Place the caps on a baking sheet.

Finely chop the stems, using only the moistest part of the stem that comes from within the cap.

Melt the butter in a skillet set over medium heat. Add the stems, green onions, and garlic. Cook for 5 minutes or until the ingredients soften. Stir in the cream cheese, salt, and pepper. Continue cooking until the mixture is heated through.

Place a heaping spoonful of the filling in the cavity of each cap. Bake for 20 minutes.

Cool the mushrooms for 5 minutes prior to serving.

▸ Kingsville Mushroom Farms, located in the town next door to Harrow, supplies a variety of mushrooms to markets throughout Canada and the United States.

▸ The freshest button mushrooms have caps that are tightly closed around their stems.

stuffed zucchini flowers

This is a traditional Italian dish, but it's perfectly suited to our area because of the local penchant for zucchini. In Italian, it's called fiori di zucca fritti, *which translates as fried zucchini flowers stuffed with mozzarella.* Serves 4.

12 zucchini flowers
½ cup (125 mL) fresh mozzarella, cut
    into ½-inch (1 cm) cubes
2 large eggs
1 cup (250 mL) all-purpose flour
1 tsp (5 mL) fine sea salt
½ tsp (2 mL) freshly ground black
    pepper
Vegetable oil, for frying

Gently open each flower and stuff with a few cubes of mozzarella. Gently twist the tip of the flower together to contain the ingredients.

Beat the eggs in a shallow bowl. Mix together the flour, salt, and pepper in a second shallow bowl.

Dip a flower into the egg mixture and allow any excess to drip off before coating it in the flour mixture. Set aside on a serving plate. Repeat for the remaining flowers.

Add oil to a skillet until it is ½ inch (1 cm) in depth. Heat the oil to 375°F (190°C).

Place as many blossoms in the skillet as possible, without overcrowding the pan. Fry for 1 minute on each side or until the blossom is golden brown. Transfer the fried flowers to a platter lined with paper towels to drain.

Sprinkle with additional salt and serve immediately.

The flowers are excellent when dipped into warm Tomato & Basil Sauce (page 23).

other fillings

Mozzarella & anchovies
Mozzarella & cherry tomatoes
Ricotta & sage
Ricotta & mint

▶ Zucchini flowers are not very common at local farm stands, but they're easy to find in local gardens when zucchini is in season late in the summer. As every gardener knows, even two plants can yield dozens of zucchini, so sacrificing a few blossoms to make this dish will hardly make a dent in the harvest.

SOUPS, SALADS, & SANDWICHES

seven-strata salad

tomato salad

bulgur salad

coleslaw

potato salad

SANDWICHES

roast beef & red onion
  marmalade sandwich

farm stand sandwich

tomato, mozzarella, & pesto
  sandwich

pulled barbecue chicken
  on a bun

meatball sub

summer pea soup

Fresh peas and mint are a winning combination. This recipe can be ready in about 30 minutes, making it a quick soup for serving at a summer lunch or dinner. Serves 4.

2 Tbsp (30 mL) unsalted butter
1 cup (250 mL) chopped yellow onion
3 cups (750 mL) fresh green peas
3 cups (750 mL) water
¼ cup (60 mL) chopped fresh mint
1 tsp (5 mL) fine sea salt
¼ tsp (1 mL) freshly ground
     black pepper

Melt the butter in a large stockpot set over medium heat. Add the onion and cook for 5 minutes or until translucent.

Add the peas and stir in the 3 cups (750 mL) water. Bring the soup to a boil over high heat. Reduce the heat to medium and cook for 10 minutes.

Add the mint, salt, and pepper. Blend the soup in a food processor until smooth. Strain the soup back into the stockpot using a sieve.

Serve hot.

▶ For a richer soup, the 3 cups (750 mL) water can be replaced with an equal amount of vegetable stock or chicken stock.

▶ Frozen green peas, thawed, can replace fresh green peas when they are out of season.

chilled tomato & cucumber soup

This simple, refreshing soup is summer in a bowl. Serves 4.

4 cups (1 L) fresh chopped tomatoes
½ tsp (2 mL) minced garlic
1 cup (250 mL) finely diced cucumber
½ cup (125 mL) finely diced sweet
    red pepper
2 Tbsp (30 mL) finely diced red onion
2 Tbsp (30 mL) red wine vinegar
1 tsp (5 mL) fine sea salt
¼ tsp (1 mL) freshly ground black
    pepper
2 tsp (10 mL) finely chopped fresh
    flat-leaf parsley

Chop the tomatoes and garlic in a food processor until smooth. Transfer the mixture to a large bowl.

Stir in the cucumber, red pepper, and red onion. Stir in the vinegar, salt, pepper, and parsley.

Chill for 2 hours before serving.

roasted field tomato soup

For years, our Aunt Linda and Uncle Joe Pavao grew tomatoes (and other vegetables) just east of Kingsville. Virtually everything on their 100-acre (40 hectare) farm was done by hand. Bushels of vine-ripened tomatoes found their way to our house every summer—they would have been ideal in this savoury soup. Serves 4.

6 field tomatoes, seeded and
    quartered
1 yellow onion, chopped
1 Tbsp (15 mL) fresh thyme
3 Tbsp (45 mL) extra virgin olive oil
1½ tsp (7 mL) fine sea salt
¾ tsp (4 mL) freshly ground black
    pepper
2 cups (500 mL) chicken stock
1 Tbsp (15 mL) finely chopped fresh
    flat-leaf parsley

Preheat the oven to 375°F (190°C).

Place the tomatoes, onion, and thyme on a large baking sheet lined with parchment paper. Drizzle the ingredients with olive oil. Sprinkle with salt and pepper, and stir to combine. Roast for 45 minutes, stirring occasionally.

Transfer the tomato mixture to a large stockpot and stir in the chicken stock. Bring to a boil over high heat, then reduce the heat to low and cook for 15 minutes.

Blend the soup in a food processor until smooth. Pour the soup through a sieve back into the stockpot. Simmer over low heat for 5 minutes. Adjust the seasonings to taste, and stir in the parsley.

Serve hot.

great lakes chowder

Lake Erie's unique ecological characteristics and rigorous government regulations have allowed a local fishing industry that's both prosperous and sustainable. For this chowder we recommend using either of Lake Erie's most famous fish: perch or pickerel. Serves 4.

2 cups (500 mL) peeled and diced
    potatoes
6 cups (1.5 L) water
1 Tbsp (15 mL) fine sea salt
3 cups (750 mL) reserved potato water
½ lb (250 g) bacon, diced
2 Tbsp (30 mL) unsalted butter
1 cup (250 mL) chopped yellow onion
1 cup (250 mL) chopped leeks
    (see note)
½ cup (125 mL) chopped celery
½ tsp (2 mL) chili flakes
⅓ cup (80 mL) all-purpose flour
1 cup (250 mL) clam juice
1 cup (250 mL) dry white wine
2 bay leaves
3 sprigs fresh thyme
1 cup (250 mL) fresh corn kernels
1 lb (500 g) fresh Lake Erie fish fillets,
    cut into 1-inch (2.5 cm) cubes
¼ cup (60 mL) finely chopped
    fresh parsley
½ cup (125 mL) whipping cream
½ tsp (2 mL) fine sea salt
¼ tsp (1 mL) fresh ground
    black pepper

Cook the diced potatoes in 6 cups (1.5 L) boiling water and 1 Tbsp (15 mL) salt. When the potatoes are tender, remove them from the water and set aside. Reserve the 3 cups (750 mL) potato water for the soup broth.

Cook the diced bacon until crisp in a large stockpot set over medium-high heat. Add the butter. When melted, stir in the onion, leeks, celery, and chili flakes. Cook for 5 minutes over medium heat or until softened.

Stir in the flour and continue cooking for 3 minutes. Stir in the clam juice, reserved potato water, wine, bay leaves, and thyme. Cook over medium heat, stirring occasionally, for 20 minutes.

Stir in the cooked potatoes, corn kernels, and fresh fish. Simmer over low heat for 5 minutes or until the fish pieces are cooked through. Stir in the parsley, cream, salt, and pepper.

Serve hot.

▶ Leeks often contain sand. To clean them, cut leeks in half lengthwise and rinse thoroughly under cold running water before chopping.

THE
HARROW
FAIR

authors'
FAVE

cream of mushroom & tarragon soup

This soup is about as far as you can get from opening a can of cream of mushroom soup. The fresh tarragon pairs beautifully with the earthiness of the mushrooms.

Serves 4.

¼ cup (60 mL) unsalted butter
3 cups (750 mL) chopped
    yellow onion
1 cup (250 mL) chopped celery
1 cup (250 mL) chopped carrots
1 tsp (5 mL) minced garlic
8 cups (2 L) chopped white and
    brown mushrooms
¼ cup (60 mL) all-purpose flour
4 cups (1 L) chicken stock
¼ cup (60 mL) dry white wine
1 cup (250 mL) whipping cream
½ cup (125 mL) finely chopped
    fresh tarragon
1 Tbsp (15 mL) fresh lemon juice
1½ tsp (7 mL) fine sea salt
¾ tsp (4 mL) freshly ground
    black pepper

Melt the butter in a large stockpot set over medium heat. Add the onion, celery, and carrots. Cook for 10 minutes or until the onions are translucent.

Stir in the garlic and mushrooms. Cook for 10 minutes. Stir in the flour, mixing well, and cook for 5 minutes. Stir in the chicken stock and wine. Cook over low heat for 20 minutes.

Blend the soup in a food processor until smooth.

Return the soup to the stockpot. Stir in the cream, tarragon, lemon juice, salt, and pepper. Simmer for another 5 minutes.

Serve hot.

▶ For a vegetarian version of this soup, replace the chicken stock with vegetable stock.

▶ Once cream has been added to a soup, do not bring the soup to a boil or it will likely split (in other words, the fats will separate from the rest of the ingredients).

brown sugar vinaigrette

This recipe is our take on the house vinaigrette once served at the Rose & Thistle Tea Room in Kingsville. Their fabulous salads were served with little pitchers of dressing on the table. This vinaigrette is a great combination of sweet and savoury flavours, perfect with a Salad with Dried Cherries. Makes 2 cups (500 mL).

1 cup (250 mL) vegetable oil
⅓ cup (80 mL) apple cider vinegar
2 Tbsp (30 mL) minced shallots
½ tsp (2 mL) minced garlic
½ tsp (2 mL) Dijon mustard
½ tsp (2 mL) Worcestershire sauce
½ tsp (2 mL) fine sea salt
¼ tsp (1 mL) freshly ground black
   pepper
¼ cup (60 mL) firmly packed
   brown sugar

Place all the ingredients in the bowl of a food processor. Blend for 1 minute or until the vinaigrette is emulsified.

Serve at room temperature.

STORAGE   Store covered in the refrigerator for up to 1 week.

THE
HARROW
FAIR

authors'
FAVE

salad with dried cherries

Serve with Brown Sugar Vinaigrette (above). Serves 4 as a starter.

6 cups (1.5 L) chopped green leaf
   lettuce
½ cup (125 mL) crumbled blue cheese
⅓ cup (80 mL) dried cherries
¼ cup (60 mL) thinly sliced red onion
¼ cup (60 mL) Brown Sugar
   Vinaigrette

Toss all the ingredients together until well coated with the vinaigrette.

Serve immediately.

creamy cucumber dressing

This is a very kid-friendly salad dressing that may even elicit requests for seconds. Try it with spinach salad. Makes 1½ cups (375 mL).

1 cup (250 mL) peeled, seeded, and
    shredded cucumber
½ cup (125 mL) milk
½ cup (125 mL) mayonnaise (page 85)
2 Tbsp (30 mL) finely chopped fresh
    tarragon
1 Tbsp (15 mL) white wine vinegar
1 tsp (5 mL) fine sea salt
½ tsp (2 mL) granulated sugar
½ tsp (2 mL) freshly ground black
    pepper

Squeeze any excess liquid from the shredded cucumber. Mix together all the ingredients in a medium-sized bowl.

Refrigerate the dressing for at least 1 hour before serving to allow the flavours to mingle.

STORAGE   Store covered in the refrigerator for up to 4 days.

spinach salad

Serve with Creamy Cucumber Dressing above. Serves 4 as a starter.

12 fresh asparagus stalks
6 cups (1.5 L) fresh baby spinach
¼ cup (60 mL) thinly sliced green
    onions
1 cup (250 mL) fresh spring pea
    shoots
½ cup (125 mL) Creamy Cucumber
    Dressing (above)

Bring a large pot of salted water to boil. Prepare an ice water bath (see note on page 12). Blanch the asparagus for 3 minutes then plunge into the ice water. Drain and set aside.

Set out 4 salad plates. Arrange 1½ cups (375 mL) spinach, 1 Tbsp (15 mL) green onions, ¼ cup (60 mL) pea shoots, and 3 stalks blanched asparagus on each plate. Drizzle each salad with the dressing.

Serve immediately.

green & yellow bean salad

In most cases, eating bean salads is like swimming in Lake Erie in January: best avoided unless serious money is involved. But this salad, made with fresh beans, requires no bribing to enjoy. Serves 4 to 6.

SALAD

½ lb (250 g) fresh yellow beans, stems trimmed

½ lb (250 g) fresh green beans, stems trimmed

1 shallot, thinly sliced into individual rings

DRESSING

¼ cup (60 mL) extra virgin olive oil

2 Tbsp (30 mL) fresh lemon juice

1 tsp (5 mL) Dijon mustard

1 tsp (5 mL) fine sea salt

½ tsp (2 mL) freshly ground black pepper

Bring a large pot of salted water to boil. Prepare an ice water bath (see note on page 12). Blanch the yellow and green beans for 3 minutes or until brightly coloured and just tender. Plunge the beans into the ice water. Once cooled, drain the beans well.

Transfer the beans to a serving bowl. Add shallots.

Whisk together the olive oil, lemon juice, mustard, salt, and pepper in a small bowl. Drizzle the dressing over the salad and gently toss to coat.

Serve chilled.

▶ Yellow beans are also known as wax beans or yellow wax beans.

▶ Shallots, though a member of the onion family, are sweeter and milder. They resemble heads of garlic with a number of bulbs clustered together at the root. The flesh of shallots has a purplish-pink tinge.

seven-strata salad

This great-tasting, great-looking salad is always the most popular item at summer picnics. And it's a cinch to make. Serves 6 to 8.

4 cups (1 L) loosely packed baby
    spinach
6 large eggs, hard-boiled and cut into
    ¼-inch (6 mm) slices (page 84)
1 tsp (5 mL) fine sea salt
½ tsp (2 mL) freshly ground black
    pepper
½ lb (250 g) bacon, diced and cooked
    until crispy
3 cups (750 mL) fresh green peas,
    blanched
¾ cup (185 mL) finely chopped
    red onion
¾ cup (185 mL) mayonnaise (page 85)
¼ cup (60 mL) herb pesto (page 17)
1 cup (250 mL) shredded aged
    Canadian cheddar cheese

Place the spinach in an 8-inch (20 cm) straight-sided, clear glass bowl. Place the egg slices on the spinach and sprinkle with half of the salt and pepper, then place the cooked bacon on the eggs.

Add layers of peas and onion. Sprinkle the onion with the remaining salt and pepper.

Mix together the mayonnaise and herb pesto in a small bowl. Spread the mixture evenly on the onion. Sprinkle the cheese evenly on the mayonnaise.

Cover and refrigerate for at least 2 hours and up to 24 hours before serving.

STORAGE Store any leftover salad, covered, in the refrigerator for up to 3 days.

tomato salad

This simple salad is a great accompaniment to almost any main course—Pan-Fried Perch (page 136), Colchester Fried Chicken (page 131), you name it. We like making it with cherry tomatoes, but larger tomatoes will work if they're cut into bite-sized pieces. (Pictured on page 112.) Serves 4 to 6.

2 cups (500 mL) halved red cherry tomatoes

2 cups (500 mL) halved yellow cherry tomatoes

½ tsp (2 mL) minced garlic

¼ cup (60 mL) chopped fresh flat-leaf parsley

⅓ cup (80 mL) extra virgin olive oil

2 Tbsp (30 mL) fresh lemon juice

1 tsp (5 mL) fine sea salt

½ tsp (2 mL) freshly ground black pepper

Place the tomatoes, garlic, and parsley in a serving bowl. Whisk together the olive oil, lemon juice, salt, and pepper in a small bowl. Pour the dressing over the salad and toss to combine. Serve immediately.

▶ Local tomatoes that work well in this recipe include grape tomatoes, pear tomatoes, and Roma tomatoes.

bulgur salad

This is our version of the classic Middle Eastern dish tabbouleh. We prefer to put everything together at the last minute for a fresh, green, lemony salad. Serves 4 to 6.

1 cup (250 mL) boiling water
1 cup (250 mL) dry bulgur
1 English cucumber
½ cup (125 mL) thinly sliced red
    onion
1 cup (250 mL) chopped fresh
    flat-leaf parsley
1 cup (250 mL) chopped fresh
    cilantro
¼ cup (60 mL) fresh lemon juice
¼ cup (60 mL) extra virgin olive oil
1 tsp (5 mL) fine sea salt
½ tsp (2 mL) freshly ground
    black pepper

Pour the boiling water over the bulgur in a medium-sized bowl. Soak the bulgur for 30 minutes or until it has softened and doubled in volume. Transfer the bulgur to the bottom of a clear serving bowl.

Cut the cucumber in half. Seed the cucumber and cut into ½-inch (1 cm) slices. Place the cucumber, onion, parsley, and cilantro on top of the bulgur.

Chill until ready to serve.

Whisk together the lemon juice, olive oil, salt, and pepper in a small bowl. Pour this dressing over the salad and toss to combine.

Serve immediately.

▶ For a more traditional bulgur salad, add 1 cup (250 mL) halved grape tomatoes and ½ cup (125 mL) crumbled Canadian feta cheese on top of the cucumber layer.

▶ For a tabbouleh with more mingled flavours, mix all the ingredients together up to 2 hours before serving.

coleslaw

Who doesn't appreciate great coleslaw served at a summer barbecue? This classic recipe comes from our grandmother, Bertha McDonald, who was a resident of Harrow for more than 60 years. Her coleslaw was a fixture at our family gatherings every summer. We've never found a version we like better. Serves 4 to 6.

5 cups (1.25 L) shredded green
  cabbage
1 cup (250 mL) shredded carrots
1 cup (250 mL) finely chopped
  red onion
½ cup (125 mL) mayonnaise (page 85)
⅓ cup (80 mL) red wine vinegar
½ tsp (2 mL) celery seeds
1 tsp (5 mL) fine sea salt
½ tsp (2 mL) freshly ground black
  pepper

Mix the cabbage, carrots, and onion together in a large bowl.

Whisk together the mayonnaise, vinegar, celery seeds, salt, and pepper in a separate bowl. Add this dressing to the vegetables and stir to combine.

Cover and refrigerate until ready to serve.

STORAGE   This recipe can be made up to 2 days ahead of time. The longer it is allowed to marinate, the more the flavours will meld together.

▶ The green cabbage and carrots in this recipe can be shredded by a food processor fitted with the grater attachment.

potato salad

Everyone loves this classic summer salad. This recipe makes great use of fresh ingredients.
Serves 4 to 6.

2 lb (1 kg) new red-skinned potatoes
½ cup (125 mL) finely diced celery
½ cup (125 mL) thinly sliced radishes
5 large eggs, hard-boiled and roughly chopped (page 84)
¾ cup (375 mL) thinly sliced green onions
2 Tbsp (30 mL) finely chopped fresh dill
2 Tbsp (30 mL) finely chopped fresh flat-leaf parsley
1 cup (250 mL) mayonnaise (page 85)
1 Tbsp (15 mL) grainy mustard
½ tsp (2 mL) fine sea salt
¼ tsp (1 mL) freshly ground black pepper

Place the potatoes in a large pot filled with cold, salted water. Bring to a boil. Reduce heat to medium-low and cook for 15 minutes or until tender.

Drain the potatoes in a large colander. Let them cool completely before cutting into bite-sized pieces. Place in a large serving bowl. Stir in the celery, radishes, chopped eggs, green onions, dill, and parsley.

Mix together the mayonnaise, grainy mustard, salt, and pepper in a small bowl. Add this dressing to the potato mixture. Stir well to combine.

Cover and refrigerate until ready to serve.

▶ Radishes add a slight crunch and a mild spiciness to this recipe. They are available at most local farm stands.

roast beef & red onion marmalade sandwich

Freshly roasted beef and Red Onion Marmalade (page 18) are the keys to the savoury-sweet goodness of this sandwich. Serve with potato salad (facing page) for a delicious lunch. Serves 4.

ROAST BEEF

1½ lb (750 g) top sirloin or rump roast
½ tsp (2 mL) fine sea salt
¼ tsp (1 mL) freshly ground black pepper
1 tsp (5 mL) vegetable oil

SANDWICHES

4 large crusty buns
½ cup (125 mL) mayonnaise (page 85)
Fine sea salt, to taste
Freshly ground black pepper, to taste
4 slices aged Canadian cheddar cheese
8 lettuce leaves
¾ cup (185 mL) Red Onion Marmalade (page 18)

ROAST BEEF

Preheat the oven to 400°F (200°C). Heat a cast iron skillet on high heat.

Sprinkle the beef with the salt and pepper. When the pan is very hot, add the oil and the beef, turning every couple of minutes until each side is browned.

Place the skillet in the oven and continue to roast the beef for 15 to 20 minutes, or until the meat has reached an internal temperature of 145°F (63°C).

Remove from the oven and loosely cover with aluminum foil for at least 10 minutes or until cool.

Slice thinly and divide into 4 equal portions.

ASSEMBLY

Cut the buns in half and spread each bottom with 2 Tbsp (30 mL) mayonnaise. Layer each bottom bun with a portion of roast beef sprinkled with salt and pepper, a slice of cheese, 2 leaves of lettuce, and 3 Tbsp (45 mL) Red Onion Marmalade.

Add the top bun to complete each sandwich.

Serve immediately.

STORAGE The sandwiches can be wrapped individually in plastic wrap and kept overnight in the refrigerator.

farm stand sandwich

This sandwich is made from late-summer veggies that appear at local farm stands. It's perfect for packing into a picnic basket. Serves 4.

VEGETABLES

1 small zucchini

1 small eggplant

1 sweet red pepper

1 medium red onion

1 cup (250 mL) grape tomatoes

⅓ cup (80 mL) extra virgin olive oil

3 Tbsp (45 mL) balsamic vinegar

1 tsp (5 mL) fine sea salt

½ tsp (2 mL) freshly ground black
    pepper

SCALLION GOAT CHEESE

½ cup (125 mL) cream cheese,
    softened

½ cup (125 mL) unripened goat
    cheese, softened

½ cup (125 mL) finely chopped
    green onions

¼ tsp (1 mL) freshly ground black
    pepper

1 large baguette

Preheat the oven to 400°F (200°C).

Cut the zucchini into ¼-inch (6 mm) slices. Peel the eggplant and cut into ¼-inch (6 mm) slices. Seed the pepper and cut into 1-inch (2.5 cm) strips. Cut the onion in half and slice into 1-inch (2.5 cm) strips lengthwise.

Toss all the chopped vegetables and tomatoes with the olive oil, balsamic vinegar, salt, and pepper in a large bowl. Spread evenly on a large baking sheet lined with parchment paper.

Roast for 30 minutes, stirring occasionally. Remove any vegetables that are golden and crisp around the edges. Continue to cook for up to 15 additional minutes, until the remaining vegetables are golden and crisp around the edges.

Cool the vegetables to room temperature. Peel the skins off pepper slices, if desired.

Meanwhile, mix together the cream cheese, goat cheese, green onions, and pepper in the bowl of a stand mixer fitted with the paddle attachment.

ASSEMBLY

Slice the baguette lengthwise. Spread half of the cheese mixture on the bottom piece of baguette and half on the top. Layer the roasted vegetables evenly over the bottom piece of baguette.

Assemble the sandwich, then slice into 4 pieces.

Serve immediately.

STORAGE The sandwiches can be wrapped individually in plastic wrap and will keep overnight in the refrigerator.

PARKS FOR A PICNIC

HOLIDAY BEACH CONSERVATION AREA

A beautiful park located along the lake, just east of Colchester.
Bird watchers of all ages enjoy the hawk observation tower.

FORT MALDEN NATIONAL PARK

Located on the shores of the Detroit River in Amherstburg, Fort
Malden is a 19th-century fortification that was used
in the War of 1812. Lots to see and do.

LAKESIDE PARK

Located just south of Kingsville's downtown area, on Lake Erie's
north shore. We highly recommend a summer picnic on a
grassy hillside overlooking the lake.

SEACLIFF PARK

Located on the shore of Lake Erie in Leamington, this pretty
park has surf, sand, and scenic spots for a picnic.

POINT PELEE NATIONAL PARK

Located southeast of Leamington, "The Point" is the southernmost
point of mainland Canada. A whole day can easily be spent
enjoying the nature trails and boardwalks. A picnic
on the beach is a must.

Pictured with Tomato Salad (page 104)

tomato, mozzarella, & pesto sandwich

In late July, bushels and baskets of tomatoes begin to appear at roadside vegetable stands around Essex County, their bright red colour beckoning passersby to stop. This sandwich really highlights the flavour of fresh, ripe tomatoes. Serves 4.

8 slices crusty white bread, ¾ inch
   (2 cm) thick
¼ cup (60 mL) extra virgin olive oil
½ cup (125 mL) basil pesto (page 16)
1 cup (250 mL) sliced fresh mozzarella
2 large fresh tomatoes, sliced

Brush one side of each slice of bread with olive oil. Spread 2 Tbsp (30 mL) of pesto evenly on 4 slices of the bread (on the side opposite the olive oil).

Place the 4 slices of bread spread with pesto (olive oil side down) into a skillet set over medium-low heat. Place a layer of cheese on top of the pesto, followed by a layer of tomatoes. Top with the remaining slices of bread (olive oil side facing out).

Grill each side for 3 minutes or until the cheese has melted and the bread is golden brown.

Serve immediately.

▶ Never store tomatoes in the refrigerator as they will quickly lose their flavour and become mealy in texture.

▶ Look for fresh mozzarella in the Italian grocery stores located around Essex County.

pulled barbecue chicken on a bun

This is the perfect sandwich to serve on a hot afternoon after going for a big swim in Lake Erie. (We suggest eating after a swim because once you eat this sandwich you'll be too full and happy to contemplate a dip.) Serves 4.

1 lb (500 g) boneless, skinless chicken breasts, cut into large chunks
1 cup (250 mL) barbecue sauce (page 21)
1 cup (250 mL) Walkerville Brewing Company's Classic Amber beer
4 large crusty rolls
¾ cup (185 mL) shredded aged Canadian cheddar cheese
¼ cup (60 mL) sliced green onions

Combine the chicken, barbecue sauce, and beer in a large saucepan set over medium-low heat. Cook for 20 minutes or until the chicken is cooked through.

Remove the chicken from the sauce and place it in a large bowl. Continue to simmer the sauce over low heat.

Using 2 forks, shred (or "pull") the chicken. Mix the pulled chicken back into the sauce and continue to simmer for 10 minutes.

Slice the rolls in half. Divide the pulled barbecue chicken among the 4 bottom halves. Sprinkle with cheese and green onions. Assemble the sandwiches.

Serve immediately.

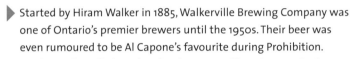 Started by Hiram Walker in 1885, Walkerville Brewing Company was one of Ontario's premier brewers until the 1950s. Their beer was even rumoured to be Al Capone's favourite during Prohibition.

The Walkerville brand and its heritage of brewing quality beer were revived in 1998. It's now the standout microbrewer of the region.

THE
HARROW
FAIR

authors'
FAVE

meatball sub

The recipe for these meatballs is from our aunt Karen Goslin. The meatballs are very versatile. Serve them as appetizers or as a main course with spaghetti. We think they're especially good served in crusty sub buns. Serves 4.

MEATBALLS

2 tsp (10 mL) minced garlic

1 cup (250 mL) fresh bread crumbs (page 137)

1 Tbsp (15 mL) finely chopped fresh flat-leaf parsley

1 tsp (5 mL) fine sea salt

½ tsp (2 mL) freshly ground black pepper

½ cup (125 mL) shredded aged Canadian cheddar cheese

1 large egg, beaten

1 lb (500 g) ground sirloin

2 Tbsp (30 mL) extra virgin olive oil

SUBS

4 cups (1 L) Tomato & Basil Sauce (page 23)

4 large crusty sub buns

2 Tbsp (30 mL) extra virgin olive oil

2 cups (500 mL) shredded mozzarella cheese

MEATBALLS

Preheat the oven to 425°F (220°C). Line a large baking sheet with parchment paper.

Place the garlic, bread crumbs, parsley, salt, pepper, cheese, and egg in a large bowl and stir until combined. Add the beef and gently mix together until just combined.

Form the meatballs into the size of golf balls, about ¼ cup (60 mL) for each ball. (Be careful not to pack the meatballs tightly or they will be too dense.) Set the meatballs onto the baking sheet. Drizzle with the olive oil.

Bake for 18 minutes, turning halfway through to brown evenly.

ASSEMBLY

Preheat the oven to broil.

Heat the Tomato & Basil Sauce in a large saucepan set over medium heat. Add the meatballs and cook until warmed through.

Line a large baking sheet with parchment paper.

Slice each of the buns in half. Brush the insides with olive oil. Place the buns on the baking sheet and toast until golden brown. Sprinkle with mozzarella, then return to the oven for 2 minutes or until the cheese is melted.

Place 4 meatballs on one side of each bun. Spoon additional sauce over the meatballs. Assemble the sub buns.

Serve immediately, with extra sauce.

MEAT

hamburgers

corn dogs

barbecued ribs

marinated lamb skewers

friday night flank steak

MAIN DISHES

POULTRY

pretzel chicken

grilled chicken wings

colchester fried chicken

turkey chili

FISH

buttered pickerel

pan-fried perch with tartar
   sauce

VEGETABLE

succotash pasta

eggplant parm'wiches

spaghetti squash with goat
   cheese & pan-fried mushrooms

hamburgers

These burgers are straight-up good. Serve them on toasted English muffins (instead of bulky buns) and set up a topping bar so the burgers can be personalized. Makes 8 burgers.

2 lb (1 kg) ground sirloin
½ cup (125 mL) finely diced
    yellow onion
2 tsp (10 mL) fine sea salt
2 tsp (10 mL) freshly ground black
    pepper
8 English muffins
¼ cup (60 mL) unsalted butter,
    softened

HAMBURGERS

Gently mix together the ground sirloin, onion, salt, and pepper in a large bowl.

Without overworking the meat, shape the mixture into 8 patties, ¼ lb (125 g) each. (The patties should be formed using a light touch and should not be firmly packed. The more imperfect and rough the patties are, the better they will taste.) Chill the patties until ready to grill.

Preheat the grill.

Grill the burgers for 4 minutes on each side or until the desired doneness is achieved. (It is essential not to press down on the burgers when grilling them. Pressing them will release the meat's juices, the very thing that makes them delicious.)

ENGLISH MUFFINS

Split the English muffins in half. Toast the English muffins until golden brown and crispy. Butter each half and cover with aluminum foil until ready to serve.

Assemble the hamburgers and add toppings!

topping bar

Pan-fried mushrooms (page 141)
Red Onion Marmalade (page 18)
Bread & butter pickles (page 28)
Dill pickles (page 26)
Pickled beets (page 31)
Blue cheese
Cheddar cheese
Leaf lettuce
Arugula
Ripe field tomatoes
Dijon mustard
Grainy mustard
Mustard relish (page 19)
Heinz ketchup
Mayonnaise (page 85)

corn dogs

When the idea of including a corn dog recipe in our cookbook first came up, we weren't sure if it would appeal to home cooks. But we tested this recipe at a dinner party and everyone loved them. With the corn dogs disappearing faster than we could make them, it felt like we were running a corn dog concession stand at, well, the Harrow Fair!

Makes 12 corn dogs.

CORNMEAL BATTER

1 cup (250 mL) milk

2 eggs

¼ cup (60 mL) vegetable oil

1 Tbsp (15 mL) granulated sugar

1¼ cups (310 mL) stone-ground
   yellow cornmeal

⅔ cup (160 mL) all-purpose flour

2 tsp (10 mL) baking powder

1 tsp (5 mL) fine sea salt

CORN DOGS

Vegetable oil, for frying

½ cup (125 mL) all-purpose flour

12 wieners

12 Popsicle sticks

CORNMEAL BATTER

Whisk together the milk, eggs, oil, and sugar in a large bowl. Mix together the cornmeal, flour, baking powder, and salt in a separate bowl.

Add the dry ingredients to the wet ingredients, stirring just until combined.

Pour the batter into a 1-quart (1 L) canning jar.

CORN DOGS

Preheat the oven to 250°F (120°C).

Add oil to a large stockpot until it is 3 inches (8 cm) in depth. Set the oil over medium-high heat until it reaches 375°F (190°C).

Spread the flour on a plate. Dry the wieners thoroughly with paper towels then roll them in the flour, coating completely. Insert a Popsicle stick into one end of each wiener, pushing it halfway in.

When the oil is hot, hold the Popsicle stick and dip the wiener into the cornmeal batter until it is completely covered. Carefully lower the corn dog into the hot oil (including the stick). Repeat with a second wiener. (It is best to cook just 2 corn dogs at a time so that the oil temperature doesn't drop too much.)

Cook the corn dogs for 2 minutes on each side or until they are golden brown. Place the fully cooked corn dogs on a baking sheet lined with paper towel and keep them warm in the oven.

Repeat the steps with the remaining wieners, ensuring that the oil comes back up to 375°F (190°C) each time.

Serve the corn dogs with ketchup, mustard, and mustard relish (page 19).

▶ Brenner wieners are our local favourite. They're made with a combination of beef and pork.

barbecued ribs

Every Labour Day weekend (for the last 43 years and counting), long before the rest of us have finished our morning coffee, the Shay family have already lit their huge grills used to cook ribs at the Harrow Fair. Over the course of the weekend, they'll grill more than 1,500 pounds (680 kilograms) of ribs for hungry attendees. For those of us cooking for smaller crowds at home, we can highly recommend our family's recipe. Serves 4 to 6.

2 whole racks of pork ribs (baby back or spare ribs), about 5 lb (2.2 kg)
2 Tbsp (30 mL) fine sea salt
1 Tbsp (15 mL) freshly ground black pepper
2 cups (500 mL) diced tomatoes
2 Tbsp (30 mL) minced garlic
2 cups (500 mL) barbecue sauce (page 21)

Preheat the oven to 350°F (180°C).

Cut the racks into thirds. Sprinkle both sides with salt and pepper. Place the ribs in a roasting pan and cover with the diced tomatoes and garlic.

Cover the roasting pan and bake for 1½ hours or until tender. Remove the ribs and discard the tomato and garlic mixture.

Preheat the grill.

Place the ribs on the hot grill, watching them carefully and turning them occasionally. After 10 minutes, brush the ribs with the barbecue sauce and grill for an additional 1 to 2 minutes. (Once the sauce is on the ribs, they will burn quickly if they aren't closely watched.)

Serve immediately.

marinated lamb skewers

This marinade is based on a Middle Eastern herb and spice mixture called charmoula. *The lamb skewers make for a great summer dinner when served with our bulgur salad (page 105).* Makes 12 skewers.

MARINADE
⅓ cup (80 mL) fresh lemon juice
½ cup (125 mL) chopped fresh
    flat-leaf parsley
½ cup (125 mL) chopped fresh
    cilantro
4 garlic cloves, peeled and crushed
2½ tsp (12 mL) fine sea salt
2 tsp (10 mL) ground cumin
1 tsp (5 mL) ground coriander
1 tsp (5 mL) paprika
½ tsp (2 mL) cayenne pepper
½ cup (125 mL) extra virgin olive oil

SKEWERS
2 lb (1 kg) boneless leg of lamb, cut
    into 1-inch (2.5 cm) cubes
2 sweet red peppers, cut into 1-inch
    (2.5 cm) pieces
1 red onion, cut into 1-inch (2.5 cm)
    pieces

MARINADE
Place all the ingredients except the olive oil in a food processor and blend until a smooth paste is created. Add the oil and mix until thoroughly combined.

Pour the mixture over the lamb cubes, tossing thoroughly until all the lamb is covered. Marinate, covered, in the refrigerator for at least 2 hours and up to 24 hours.

ASSEMBLY
Soak twelve 8-inch (20 cm) wooden skewers in hot water for 30 minutes before using.

Skewer pieces of lamb alternately with pieces of pepper and onion. Preheat the grill.

Grill the lamb for 3 minutes per side or until medium-rare. Serve immediately.

THE
HARROW
FAIR

authors'
FAVE

Pictured with Bulgur Salad (page 105)

friday night flank steak

Friday nights during the summer have a quality that should be bottled. A weekend full of fun possibilities lies ahead, and making a complicated dinner is the last thing on anyone's agenda. But with a little advance preparation, and some great music, dinner will be flavourful and fun. Serves 4 to 6.

2 lb (1 kg) flank steak
½ cup (125 mL) vegetable oil
½ cup (125 mL) red wine vinegar
½ cup (125 mL) chopped red onion
2 Tbsp (30 mL) minced garlic
1 Tbsp (15 mL) fine sea salt
1 tsp (5 mL) freshly ground black
    pepper
1 tsp (5 mL) dry mustard
4 sprigs fresh thyme

Begin marinating meat at least 4 hours and up to 24 hours before dinner.

Place the flank steak in a large resealable plastic bag. Whisk together the remaining ingredients in a medium-sized bowl. Pour the marinade into the bag with the steak. Seal and shake well to coat.

Store in the refrigerator for at least 4 hours, turning the bag occasionally so the steak is evenly marinated.

Remove the steak from the refrigerator 30 minutes before cooking time. Preheat the grill.

Grill the steak for 3 to 4 minutes per side or until medium-rare. Let the steak rest, covered with aluminum foil, for 10 minutes before cutting across the grain into thin slices.

Serve warm or at room temperature.

MOTOR CITY MUSIC

Harrow is 42 kilometres (26 miles) from Motown (Detroit, Michigan). Everyone who grew up in our area grew up listening to some of the best music ever created. For a fun and funky Friday night, this is our playlist:

Got to Give It Up – MARVIN GAYE • *Don't Leave Me This Way* – THELMA HOUSTON • *Lovely Day* – BILL WITHERS • *Shop Around* – THE MIRACLES • *I Say a Little Prayer* – ARETHA FRANKLIN • *I Want You Back* – THE JACKSON FIVE • *Ain't No Woman (Like the One I've Got)* – FOUR TOPS • *Brick House* – THE COMMODORES • *Superstition* – STEVIE WONDER • *Nowhere to Run* – MARTHA AND THE VANDELLAS • *You Keep Me Hangin' On* – THE SUPREMES • *Money (That's What I Want)* – BARRETT STRONG • *My Guy* – MARY WELLS • *Ain't No Mountain High Enough* – MARVIN GAYE & TAMMI TERRELL • *Uptight (Everything's Alright)* – STEVIE WONDER • *I Can't Help Myself* – THE FOUR TOPS • *I'm Coming Out* – DIANA ROSS • *Use Me* – BILL WITHERS • *Papa Was a Rollin' Stone* – THE TEMPTATIONS • *This Old Heart of Mine* – THE ISLEY BROTHERS •

pretzel chicken

Pretzels are an everyday snack food, but this delicious dish elevates them to new heights. Serve with our Green & Yellow Bean Salad (page 101). Serves 4.

¼ cup (60 mL) vegetable oil
¼ cup (60 mL) grainy mustard
1 Tbsp (15 mL) Dijon mustard
1 Tbsp (15 mL) yellow mustard
¼ cup (60 mL) freshly squeezed
    orange juice
1 Tbsp (15 mL) white wine vinegar
½ tsp (2 mL) fine sea salt
¼ tsp (1 mL) freshly ground black
    pepper
4 boneless, skinless chicken
    breast halves, cut into thirds
    lengthwise
4 cups (1 L) crushed hard pretzels
    (approx)

Preheat the oven to 400°F (200°C). Line a large baking sheet with parchment paper and set aside.

Whisk together the oil, mustards, orange juice, vinegar, salt, and pepper in a large, shallow bowl. Coat the chicken evenly with the sauce. Allow the chicken to marinate in the refrigerator for 1 hour or up to 24 hours.

Place the crushed pretzels in a second large, shallow bowl. Press the chicken pieces in the crushed pretzels until well coated. Place the chicken on the prepared baking sheet.

Bake for 30 minutes or until the chicken is cooked through. Serve warm.

▶ Crush the pretzels in a food processor. A mix of fine crumbs and larger chunks is ideal.

grilled chicken wings

Grilling is our preferred cooking method for wings; a crispy skin can be achieved without the use of a deep fryer. The dark, smoky flavours of the spices in this recipe are enhanced with fresh lime juice at the end. Serves 4 to 6.

2 Tbsp (30 mL) paprika
1 Tbsp (15 mL) firmly packed brown
   sugar
2 tsp (10 mL) fine sea salt
1 tsp (5 mL) chili powder
1 tsp (5 mL) dry mustard
1 tsp (5 mL) ground cumin
½ tsp (2 mL) cayenne pepper
½ tsp (2 mL) freshly ground black
   pepper
3 lb (1.5 kg) chicken wings
2 limes, one of them cut into wedges

Mix all the dry ingredients together in a large bowl. Add the chicken wings and stir to coat thoroughly. Marinate the wings in the refrigerator for at least 1 hour and up to 24 hours.

Bring the wings up to room temperature 30 minutes prior to grilling. Preheat the grill.

Grill the wings until cooked through and crispy (but still juicy), turning often to avoid scorching.

Squeeze 1 lime over the wings just prior to serving.

Serve immediately with lime wedges.

colchester fried chicken

Colchester is the village south of Harrow. Its pretty harbour attracts boaters during the summer, and there are plenty of spots to enjoy a picnic along the waterfront. Why not make it an event? Put Colchester Fried Chicken, Potato Salad (page 108), and Rustic Fruit Tarts (page 174) on the menu. Serves 4 to 6.

1 whole fresh chicken
3½ cups (875 mL) all-purpose flour, divided
2 cups (500 mL) buttermilk (see note on page 49)
1 Tbsp + 1½ tsp (15 mL + 7 mL) fine sea salt, divided
¼ cup (60 mL) firmly packed fresh sage
1 tsp (5 mL) freshly ground black pepper
1 tsp (5 mL) smoked paprika
Vegetable oil, for frying

THE HARROW FAIR

authors' FAVE

Cut the chicken into pieces: 2 legs, 2 thighs, 2 wings, 2 breasts. Cut each breast into 3 equal pieces. Discard the back or save for another use.

Whisk together ½ cup (125 mL) of the flour, the buttermilk, and the 1 Tbsp (15 mL) salt in a large bowl. Rub the sage leaves between your hands to release the aroma of the herb and add to the buttermilk mixture.

Place all the chicken pieces in the buttermilk mixture. Stir to coat thoroughly. Refrigerate the chicken for at least 2 hours and up to 24 hours.

Mix together 3 cups (750 mL) of the flour, the 1½ tsp (7 mL) salt, pepper, and paprika in a large bowl.

Firmly press the flour mixture into the chicken pieces, one at a time, until they are thoroughly coated. (This is an essential step to getting perfect fried chicken.)

In a large, straight-sided saucepan or skillet, heat 1 inch (2.5 cm) of oil to 350°F (180°C). Fit all the chicken pieces into the oil. (The chicken does not need to be covered by the oil.) Cover and cook over medium heat for 10 minutes on one side, then 10 minutes on the other. Remove the lid and cook the chicken for an additional 2 minutes or until it is a dark, golden brown.

Place the fried chicken pieces on a baking sheet lined with paper towels.

Let the chicken rest for 15 minutes before serving.

turkey chili

Turkey Chili is the perfect dish to serve to a crowd. Set up a topping bar so bowls of chili can be personalized. Serves 4 to 6.

2 Tbsp (30 mL) sunflower oil
1 cup (250 mL) chopped yellow onion
4 garlic cloves, minced
1 lb (500 g) ground turkey
2 Tbsp (30 mL) chili powder
1 Tbsp (15 mL) ground cumin
⅛ tsp (0.5 mL) cayenne pepper
6 cups (1.5 L) chopped fresh tomatoes
2 roasted sweet red peppers,
    chopped
2 cups (500 mL) cooked black beans
2 cups (500 mL) cooked kidney beans
1 cup (250 mL) fresh corn kernels
1 tsp (5 mL) fine sea salt
½ tsp (2 mL) freshly ground
    black pepper

Place the oil in a large stockpot set over high heat. Add the onion and garlic and cook over medium heat for 10 minutes.

Add the turkey and cook until it is no longer pink.

Stir in the chili powder, cumin, and cayenne pepper. Add the tomatoes, roasted peppers, beans, and corn kernels.

Simmer over medium-low heat for 45 minutes, stirring occasionally.

Add salt and pepper and adjust to taste.

Serve warm.

topping bar

Tortilla chips
Aged Canadian cheddar cheese
Fresh cilantro
Green onions
Pickled jalapeños
Sour cream
Lime wedges

quick-cooking dried beans

1 cup (250 mL) dried beans
(makes about 2 cups/500 mL
cooked beans)

Place the beans in a large saucepan and cover with 1 inch (2.5 cm) cold water. Bring the water to a boil and cook for 2 minutes. Turn off the heat and cover the pan with a lid.

Let the beans sit for 1 hour, or up to 3 hours.

Drain the water from the saucepan and replace it with fresh, cold water. Bring the water to a boil, then reduce to low heat and simmer for 30 to 45 minutes or until the beans are tender.

▶ For the last 100 years, the Harrow Research Station has been making major contributions to Canadian agriculture. Today, the station employs 200 people, many of whom are research scientists focused on developing sustainable land and crop management strategies. They also concentrate on environmental quality, pest management, and developing new varietals of fruits and vegetables.

Many of the peaches, apricots, pears, nectarines, cucumbers, and beans (like the black beans and kidney beans used in this recipe) enjoyed by consumers around the country were developed in Harrow.

Our friend Jimmy Lypps is Harrow Research Station's "chief bean cooker." Responsible for all bean processing, Jimmy conducts side-by-side comparisons of beans to determine which varieties will make their way to market and which are in need of further development.

buttered pickerel

This is the best method we've ever come across for baking fresh fish. If the steps are followed, the fish will come out perfectly every time. Buttered Lake Erie pickerel is fabulous when paired with herb pesto (page 17). Serves 4.

4 Tbsp (60 mL) unsalted butter,
    softened, divided
2 Tbsp (30 mL) water
4 pickerel fillets, about 8 oz
    (250 g) each
1 Tbsp (15 mL) fine sea salt
2 tsp (10 mL) freshly ground
    black pepper

Preheat the oven to 400°F (200°C).

Coat the bottom of a large skillet with 2 Tbsp (30 mL) of the butter. Sprinkle the surface of the skillet with 2 Tbsp (30 mL) water. Set aside.

Ensure the pickerel fillets have been thoroughly deboned and skinned. Sprinkle both sides of each fillet with salt and pepper.

Place the fillets in the pan. Dot the top of the fillets with the remaining 2 Tbsp (30 mL) butter.

Set the skillet over high heat, bringing the water to a boil. Immediately transfer the pan to the oven and bake for 7 minutes or until the fish is opaque and flaky.

Serve immediately.

▶ The western basin of Lake Erie is the largest producer of freshwater fish in North America.

pan-fried perch

Growing up on the lake gave us plenty of opportunities to go fishing. Occasionally we were lucky enough to catch a perch (or anything at all, for that matter). Native to Lake Erie, perch is our choice for our mom's excellent breaded fish recipe. Ideally, make your own bread crumbs for this recipe, and be sure to serve the fish with generous portions of tartar sauce (both recipes facing page). Serves 4.

2 lb (1 kg) Lake Erie perch fillets
1 cup (250 mL) all-purpose flour
2 tsp (10 mL) fine sea salt
1 tsp (5 mL) freshly ground black
    pepper
3 large eggs
2 cups (500 mL) bread crumbs
    (facing page)
1 Tbsp (15 mL) chopped fresh flat-leaf
    parsley
Vegetable oil, for frying

THE
HARROW
FAIR

———

authors'
FAVE

Preheat the oven to 225°F (105°C).

Set out 3 shallow bowls for use in breading the fillets. In the first bowl, combine the flour, salt, and pepper. In the second bowl, beat the eggs well. In the third bowl, stir together the bread crumbs and parsley.

Heat ½ inch (1 cm) of the oil in a skillet set over medium-high heat.

Coat the perch pieces in the flour, dip into the beaten eggs, and then coat with the bread crumb mixture, pressing to make sure the crumbs will stay on.

Add the fillets to the hot oil, but do not overcrowd. Cook one side for 3 to 4 minutes before turning over and cooking for another 3 to 4 minutes. Be sure to watch the fish carefully as it will burn if the oil is too hot. The fish is ready when the bread crumbs are uniformly golden brown in colour and the flesh easily flakes when touched by a fork.

Once fried, place the fillets on a baking sheet lined with paper towel to drain, and keep in the oven until the remaining pieces are completed.

Repeat until all remaining fillets are cooked, making sure to keep the oil level at ½ inch (1 cm).

Serve immediately.

▶ If you haven't gone to the trouble of obtaining a fishing licence and catching your own, the best place to buy fresh perch in our area is at the Kingsville Dock.

Commercial fishing boats work on Lake Erie year-round.

bread crumbs

Any recipe calling for bread crumbs will be improved by using bread crumbs made at home. The key is to start with a high-quality white bread that is fresh, not stale. Makes about 2 cups (500 mL).

1 loaf high-quality white bread

Preheat the oven to 325°F (160°C).

Cut the loaf into slices. (Remove the crusts if a pale bread crumb is desired.) Place the slices on a baking sheet and bake for 45 minutes or until thoroughly brittle.

Grind the bread into fine crumbs in a food processor.

STORAGE Store in an airtight container for up to 1 month.

tartar sauce

Tartar sauce is one of the things we love most about traditional fish and chips. This recipe is the perfect accompaniment to our mom's Pan-Fried Perch. Makes 1 cup (250 mL).

1 cup (250 mL) mayonnaise (page 85)
3 Tbsp (45 mL) finely diced celery
3 Tbsp (45 mL) finely diced dill pickle
2 Tbsp (30 mL) thinly sliced green onions
1 Tbsp (15 mL) finely chopped capers
1 Tbsp (15 mL) fresh lemon juice
1 tsp (5 mL) minced garlic
1 anchovy fillet, minced

Combine all the ingredients and mix well in a medium-sized bowl. Cover and refrigerate until ready to serve.

STORAGE The sauce will keep in the refrigerator for up to 1 week.

▶ Don't be tempted to omit the anchovy from this recipe. It's an ingredient that's definitely worth adding for its depth of flavour.

succotash pasta

Succotash is a Native American dish, consisting primarily of corn and lima beans or other shell beans. Lima beans are difficult (if not impossible) to find fresh in our area, so we've substituted sugar snap peas. They're a great addition to this creamy pasta dish. Serves 4.

8 oz (250 g) dried farfalle (bow-tie) pasta
4 slices bacon, diced
½ cup (125 mL) chopped yellow onion
2 cups (500 mL) fresh corn kernels
2 cups (500 mL) sugar snap peas, topped and tailed
½ cup (125 mL) whipping cream
2 Tbsp (30 mL) unsalted butter
1 tsp (5 mL) fine sea salt
½ tsp (2 mL) freshly ground black pepper
½ cup (125 mL) grated Parmesan cheese

Place the pasta in a large stockpot filled with well-salted boiling water. Cook for 8 minutes or until the pasta is tender but firm to bite. Drain the pasta, reserving 1 cup (250 mL) of the pasta water.

While the pasta is cooking, fry the bacon in a skillet set over medium heat. Remove the bacon and set aside. Pour off all the fat, but don't wipe the skillet clean.

Set the skillet over medium heat and cook the onion until soft. Stir in the bacon, corn, peas, and cream and simmer for 5 minutes.

Add the pasta to the pan. Toss all the ingredients together and cook for another 2 minutes.

Stir in the butter, salt, and pepper. If the pasta seems too dry, stir in ¼ cup (60 mL) of the reserved pasta water and simmer for an additional minute. Add more pasta water, if needed.

Top with Parmesan and serve immediately.

eggplant parm'wiches

If you've ever made eggplant Parmesan before, you'll be shocked at how easy this recipe is—and at how little oil it uses. The method has forever changed how we make this dish. Serves 4.

1 cup (250 mL) all-purpose flour

1 tsp (5 mL) kosher salt

½ tsp (2 mL) freshly ground black pepper

4 large eggs

2 cups (500 mL) bread crumbs (page 137)

1 cup (250 mL) grated Parmesan cheese, divided

¼ cup (60 mL) vegetable oil

2 to 3 medium eggplants

1 cup (250 mL) Tomato & Basil Sauce (page 23)

1 cup (250 mL) shredded mozzarella

THE
HARROW
FAIR

authors'
FAVE

Place a large baking sheet in the oven and preheat to 425°F (220°C).

Combine the flour, salt, and pepper in a shallow bowl. Beat the eggs together in a second shallow bowl. Combine the bread crumbs and ½ cup (125 mL) of the Parmesan in a third shallow bowl.

Remove the baking sheet from the oven and brush with the oil.

Cut the eggplant into 16 rounds, at least ¾ inch (2 cm) thick. Dip the eggplant rounds in the flour mixture, then the egg mixture, then the bread crumb mixture. Place slices of coated eggplant on the baking sheet as they are completed.

Bake for 15 minutes, then remove the baking sheet from the oven and turn each slice over. Return to the oven and bake for an additional 10 minutes.

After baking, place 1 to 2 Tbsp (15 to 30 mL) of Tomato & Basil Sauce on half the slices and sprinkle them with the remaining ½ cup (125 mL) Parmesan and the mozzarella. (Do not smother the rounds in sauce and cheese or they will lose their crispness while baking.)

Return the eggplant to the oven for 10 minutes or until the cheese is melted and bubbling.

Top the cheese-covered eggplant with the rounds that were left uncovered. Serve warm.

▶ Eggplant is available from Essex County farm stands beginning in July.

spaghetti squash with goat cheese

Topped with pan-fried mushrooms, this is our new favourite vegetarian main course. Skip the mushrooms and you've got a savoury side dish. Serves 4.

1 large spaghetti squash
1 bulb garlic
2 Tbsp (30 mL) extra virgin olive oil
2 tsp (10 mL) chopped fresh thyme
2 tsp (10 mL) white wine vinegar
1 tsp (5 mL) fine sea salt
½ tsp (2 mL) freshly ground black pepper
2 cups (500 mL) loosely packed arugula
½ cup (125 mL) crumbled goat cheese

Preheat the oven to 375°F (190°C). Line a large baking sheet with parchment paper.

Cut the squash in half lengthwise. Place the squash, cut side up, on the baking sheet.

Cut ¼ inch (6 mm) off of the top of the garlic bulb. Place the bulb on a square of aluminum foil. Pour 1 Tbsp (15 mL) olive oil over the top and wrap tightly in foil. Place the wrapped garlic on the baking sheet with the squash. Bake for 1 hour or until a knife can pierce the squash easily.

Scoop the seeds out of the centre of the squash and discard. Separate the flesh from the rind and place the squash in a large bowl. Discard the rind.

Unwrap the garlic and squeeze the bulb so the soft garlic cloves come out. Transfer the garlic cloves to a bowl and mash with a fork. Add the thyme, vinegar, salt, and pepper. Mix well.

Pour the garlic sauce over the squash. Gently fold in the arugula and crumbled goat cheese. Serve warm.

pan-fried mushrooms

The secret here is to sear the mushrooms in a very hot skillet for great flavour and texture. You can also try these as a topping on hamburgers (page 121). Makes 2 cups (500 mL).

1 Tbsp (15 mL) unsalted butter
1 Tbsp (15 mL) extra virgin olive oil
4 cups (1 L) sliced mushrooms
1 garlic clove, minced
¼ tsp (1 mL) fine sea salt
pinch freshly ground black pepper
2 Tbsp (30 mL) chopped fresh flat-leaf parsley

Heat the butter and oil in a large skillet over high heat. When the butter has melted and is just beginning to brown, add the mushrooms. Cook without stirring for 2 to 3 minutes or until brown.

Stir in the minced garlic, salt, and pepper. Continue to cook for an additional 5 minutes or until the mushrooms are soft and well browned. Stir in the parsley. Serve warm.

▶ Try a mixture of button, cremini, portobello, shiitake, and oyster mushrooms in this recipe.

SIDE DISHES

hand-cut fries

beer-battered onion rings

skillet-sizzled cornbread

maple baked beans

broccoli casserole

sweet corn casserole

scalloped potatoes

roasted cauliflower, carrots,
 & parsnips

corn off the cob

zucchini & tomatoes

hand-cut fries

Making perfect fries at home is easier than you'd think when using one of our favourite cooking tools—a deep-fry/candy thermometer. The secret is first blanching the cut potatoes in oil heated to 300°F (150°C), then frying them at 350°F (180°C). The insides will be soft; the outsides will be crispy and golden. In our area, there's only one condiment that's acceptable: Heinz ketchup. Serves 4.

4 large potatoes (preferably
    Yukon Gold)
Peanut oil, for frying
Fine sea salt, to taste

Peel the potatoes and cut them lengthwise into ½-inch (1 cm) thick slices, then cut them again into ½-inch (1 cm) wide sticks.

Place the sticks in a large bowl and cover with cold water. Store in refrigerator for at least 4 hours and up to 24 hours.

Drain the potatoes and dry them thoroughly with a kitchen towel just prior to frying.

Pour 3 inches (8 cm) oil in a large, heavy-bottomed pot and heat it to 300°F (150°C).

Working in small batches, lower the potatoes into the oil. Stir to separate. (The oil temperature is going to drop, but will rise again in a few minutes.) Blanch the potatoes until they are almost cooked through, but not brown. Remove the potatoes from the oil with a slotted spoon and spread them on a baking sheet lined with a paper towel to drain. Allow the oil to return to 300°F (150°C) before blanching the next batch.

When finished blanching all the potatoes, heat the oil to 350°F (180°C). Again, working in small batches, add the blanched potatoes to the oil. Fry for 2 minutes or until golden brown. Remove the fries from the oil and spread on a baking sheet lined with fresh paper towels to drain. Allow the oil to return to 350°F (180°C) between each batch.

Sprinkle the hot fries with fine sea salt.

Serve immediately with you-know-what.

▶ We recommend Yukon Gold potatoes in this recipe because they make for buttery-tasting fries. The popular cultivar was developed in Ontario at the University of Guelph.

▶ The H. J. Heinz Company established manufacturing operations in 1909 in the local town of Leamington. For a century, local growers have supplied the Heinz plant with produce: cucumbers, peppers, beans, and, most notably, tomatoes. Leamington is the largest tomato processing region per acreage in the world, making it worthy of the nickname "Tomato Capital of Canada."

beer-battered onion rings

No one we know would say no to these onion rings. Serves 4.

2 large yellow onions
Vegetable oil, for frying
½ cup (125 mL) all-purpose flour
½ cup (125 mL) cornstarch
1 tsp (5 mL) fine sea salt
½ tsp (2 mL) freshly ground black
    pepper
1 cup (250 mL) good-quality
    Canadian beer, cold
1 large egg

Slice the onions into rings, about ½ inch (1 cm) thick. Reserve the smaller inner rings for another purpose.

Pour 3 inches (8 cm) oil in a large, heavy-bottomed pot and heat it to 375°F (190°C). Preheat the oven to 250°F (120°C).

While the oil is heating, mix together the flour, cornstarch, salt, and pepper in a large bowl. Whisk in the beer and egg until smooth.

When the oil is ready, dredge a few of the onion rings in the beer batter. Shake off any excess batter before carefully placing the onions in the oil. Fry for 2 minutes on each side or until they are golden brown.

Remove the onion rings with a slotted spoon and spread them on a baking sheet lined with a paper towel to drain. Keep them in the oven until all the onion rings are complete.

Allow the oil to return to 375°F (190°C) between each batch and repeat the steps until all the onions have been fried.

Serve immediately.

skillet-sizzled cornbread

A hot pan of cornbread is fantastic any time of the year, but it is particularly satisfying when the weather turns cooler at the end of summer. Serve it with a batch of Turkey Chili (page 132). Makes 8 generous wedges.

1 cup (250 mL) stone-ground
    yellow cornmeal
1 cup (250 mL) all-purpose flour
1 Tbsp (15 mL) baking powder
¼ tsp (1 mL) fine sea salt
¼ tsp (1 mL) baking soda
1¼ cups (310 mL) buttermilk
    (see note on page 49)
1 large egg
2 Tbsp (30 mL) granulated sugar
¼ cup (60 mL) vegetable oil
3 Tbsp (45 mL) unsalted butter
1 cup (250 mL) fresh corn kernels

Preheat oven to 375°F (190°C).

Place a 10-inch (25 cm) skillet in the oven to heat. (The pan needs to be quite hot to give the cornbread a proper crust.)

Combine the cornmeal, flour, baking powder, and salt in a large bowl. Stir the baking soda into the buttermilk in a small bowl. Whisk together the egg, sugar, and oil in a third bowl. Whisk in the buttermilk mixture.

Carefully remove the hot skillet from the oven. Add the butter to the hot pan—it will melt and sizzle. Tilt the pan to coat the bottom and sides.

Quickly add the wet ingredients to the dry. Stir in the corn kernels until all the ingredients are just combined. Pour the batter into the skillet.

Immediately put the skillet in the oven and bake for 20 minutes or until golden brown.

Cut into wedges and serve right out of the pan with extra butter.

▶ Due to its southern latitude and warm climate, Essex County has the first sweet corn available in all of Canada. It can be ready in early July, up to two weeks ahead of the rest of the country.

▶ When selecting corn, the unhusked ear should feel firm, have full kernels to the top of the ear, and have brown, dry silk.

maple baked beans

If we're throwing a party in the summer, it's almost guaranteed that we'll be serving a big pot of these baked beans. The smell of bacon and maple syrup fills the air, attracting family members and curious guests hoping for a pre-party taste. Serves 8.

2 cups (500 mL) dried navy beans, cooked (see page 133)
½ lb (250 g) bacon, diced
1½ cups (375 mL) chopped yellow onion
1 bottle good quality Canadian beer
4 cups (1 L) diced fresh tomatoes
¾ cup (185 mL) Heinz ketchup
¾ cup (185 mL) pure maple syrup
⅓ cup (80 mL) firmly packed brown sugar
1 Tbsp (15 mL) dry mustard
1 tsp (5 mL) smoked paprika
1 tsp (5 mL) chili flakes
1 tsp (5 mL) fine sea salt
½ tsp (2 mL) freshly ground black pepper

Preheat the oven to 300°F (150°C).

Cook the bacon until crispy in a skillet set over medium-high heat. Place the bacon and the beans in a large stockpot, without removing the bacon fat from the skillet.

Add the onion to the skillet. Cook over medium-high heat for 5 minutes or until tender. Add the beer, scraping the bottom of the pan to remove all the crispy bits. Add the onion and beer to the beans.

Add the tomatoes, ketchup, maple syrup, brown sugar, dry mustard, smoked paprika, chili flakes, salt, and pepper to the beans. Bake covered for 2½ hours. Uncover and bake for up to 1 hour, stirring occasionally, until the sauce is thickened.

Serve warm.

▶ To cook the baked beans in a slow cooker, prepare the recipe until the bacon and onion are cooked. Transfer these to the slow cooker along with all other ingredients. Cook for 4 hours on the high setting and another 4 to 6 hours on the low setting, stirring occasionally.

THE
HARROW
FAIR

authors'
FAVE

broccoli casserole

Made with frozen broccoli, a can of cream of mushroom soup, and crackers, broccoli casserole was a very popular dish on dinner tables of the '70s and '80s. We've updated that version by using fresh ingredients. Serves 4 to 6.

12 cups (3 L) chopped fresh broccoli
¼ cup (60 mL) unsalted butter
2 cups (500 mL) sliced button
    mushrooms
1 cup (250 mL) diced yellow onion
¼ cup (60 mL) all-purpose flour
2 cups (500 mL) milk
1¾ cups (435 mL) shredded aged
    Canadian cheddar cheese,
    divided
¼ tsp (1 mL) chili flakes
1½ tsp (7 mL) fine sea salt
¼ tsp (1 mL) freshly ground black
    pepper
⅓ cup (80 mL) bread crumbs
    (page 137)

Preheat the oven to 375°F (190°C).

Fill a stockpot with water and bring to a boil. Blanch the broccoli pieces for 2 minutes or until slightly tender but still crunchy. Drain well and set aside.

Melt the butter over medium heat in a large saucepan. Cook the mushrooms and onion for 5 minutes or until softened.

Add the flour and stir for 2 minutes. Add the milk, whisking vigorously. Bring the entire mixture to a simmer.

Stir in 1½ cups (375 mL) of the cheese, chili flakes, salt, and pepper. Add the broccoli and bread crumbs. Pour the mixture into an 8- × 8-inch (20 × 20 cm) baking dish and sprinkle with the remaining ¼ cup (60 mL) cheese.

Bake for 30 minutes or until bubbling.

Serve warm.

▶ Broccoli starts appearing at local farm stands in midsummer. Seek out stalks that are a deep green colour. The buds should be tightly closed and the leaves should be crisp.

sweet corn casserole

When we were growing up, our aunt Ellen Strobel served her sweet corn casserole at every important family dinner. We experimented and came up with our own version, while keeping the spirit of her original dish. Serves 4 to 6.

3 cups (750 mL) fresh corn kernels

2 large eggs

¼ cup (60 mL) milk

½ cup (125 mL) bread crumbs
　　(page 137)

¼ cup (60 mL) unsalted butter,
　　melted

¼ cup (60 mL) grated carrots

¼ cup (60 mL) finely chopped
　　sweet red pepper

¼ cup (60 mL) finely chopped
　　yellow onion

¼ tsp (1 mL) chili flakes

½ tsp (2 mL) fine sea salt

½ cup (125 mL) shredded aged
　　Canadian cheddar cheese

Preheat oven to 350°F (180°C). Butter an 8- × 8-inch (20 × 20 cm) baking dish and set aside.

　　Pulse the corn kernels in a food processor until they are creamy, but not smooth.

　　Beat the eggs and milk together in a large bowl. Stir in the bread crumbs and set aside until all the liquid is absorbed.

　　Stir the corn, butter, carrots, red pepper, onion, chili flakes, and salt into the bread crumb mixture. Place the mixture into the baking dish. Sprinkle with the cheese.

　　Bake for 45 minutes.

　　Serve warm.

▶ It will take 4 to 5 ears of corn to make 3 cups (750 mL) of kernels. Once the kernels have been cut off, use the back of a knife to scrape the cobs to remove all the milky corn mush.

scalloped potatoes

This indulgent side dish never has leftovers. We've witnessed family and friends going back for seconds—and thirds! Serves 6 to 8.

¼ cup (60 mL) vegetable oil

8 cups (2 L) sliced yellow onion

4 lb (1.8 kg) boiling potatoes, peeled

1½ cups (375 mL) whipping cream, divided

1¼ cups (310 mL) grated Parmesan cheese, divided

2 Tbsp + 1½ tsp (30 mL + 7 mL) finely chopped fresh thyme, divided

4 tsp (20 mL) fine sea salt

1 tsp (5 mL) freshly ground black pepper

Heat the oil in a large skillet set over medium-low heat. Add the onion. Cook for about 30 minutes or until the onion has caramelized.

Preheat the oven to 350°F (180°C).

Slice the potatoes as thinly as possible and place them in a large mixing bowl. Toss the potato slices with 1 cup (250 mL) of the whipping cream, 1 cup (250 mL) of the Parmesan, the 2 Tbsp (30 mL) thyme, salt, and pepper. Fold in the caramelized onion.

Place the scalloped potatoes into a 9- × 13-inch (3.5 L) baking dish. Cover the top with the remaining ½ cup (125 mL) whipping cream, the remaining ¼ cup (60 mL) Parmesan, and the 1½ tsp (7 mL) thyme.

Cover with a lid or aluminum foil and bake for 2 hours or until a knife slides in easily.

Serve warm.

▶ Caramelized onions can be made ahead and kept in the freezer for up to 3 months.

roasted cauliflower, carrots, & parsnips

The Harrow Fair represents the unofficial end of summer. While we are sorry to see it go, this side dish makes the transition a little easier. Roasting these vegetables caramelizes their natural sugars, taking them from so-so to sublime. Serves 4 to 6.

1 medium head of cauliflower
2 cups (500 mL) peeled carrots cut
    into ½-inch (1 cm) coins
2 cups (500 mL) peeled parsnips cut
    into ½-inch (1 cm) coins
2 Tbsp (30 mL) extra virgin olive oil
1 tsp (5 mL) fine sea salt
½ tsp (2 mL) freshly ground
    black pepper

Preheat the oven to 375°F (190°C). Line a large baking sheet with parchment paper.

Cut the cauliflower into small florets. Toss the cauliflower, carrots, and parsnips with the olive oil, salt, and pepper in a large bowl. Spread the vegetables evenly on the baking sheet.

Roast for 25 minutes or until the vegetables are tender and starting to brown.

Serve warm.

corn off the cob

While our kids and husbands love corn on the cob, we find it difficult to eat without losing our dignity. This side dish keeps us presentable, and it's incredibly easy to make. The mint may seem like an odd addition, but trust us—it pairs beautifully with the buttery, caramelized corn. Serves 4.

6 fresh ears of corn
¼ cup (60 mL) unsalted butter
¼ cup (60 mL) chopped fresh mint
½ tsp (2 mL) fine sea salt
¼ tsp (1 mL) freshly ground
    black pepper

Husk the corn cobs, then cut the kernels off the cobs.

Melt the butter in a large skillet set over high heat. Add the corn and cook, stirring often, for 10 minutes or until the kernels begin to caramelize. Stir in the mint, salt, and pepper.

Transfer the corn to a serving bowl and serve immediately.

▶ Peaches & Cream sweet corn is definitely our first choice when buying local corn in the summer. And Moira's preferred technique for husking corn and removing the silks? Get someone else to do it.

zucchini & tomatoes

A simplified version of ratatouille, this recipe is a great way to use garden vegetables that can be overly abundant at the end of summer. Serves 4 to 6.

2 Tbsp (30 mL) extra virgin olive oil
1 garlic clove, minced
1 yellow onion, halved and sliced thickly
3 cups (750 mL) chopped fresh field tomatoes
1 tsp (5 mL) fine sea salt
½ tsp (2 mL) freshly ground black pepper
3 small zucchini, cut into ½-inch (1 cm) slices
2 tsp (10 mL) chopped fresh oregano

Heat the oil in a large saucepan set over medium heat. Add the garlic and onion, and cook until the onion is soft (but not brown), about 3 minutes.

Stir in the tomatoes, salt, and pepper and stir. Cook for 5 minutes. Stir in the zucchini and oregano. Continue cooking for 10 minutes or until the tomatoes are stewed and the zucchini is soft.

Serve warm.

THE
HARROW
FAIR

authors'
FAVE

CLASSIC PIES

favourite pie crust

apple pie

peaches & cream pie

rhubarb custard pie

pumpkin pie

raspberry & cherry pie

wild black raspberry &
  blueberry pie

cream pie

raisin pie

PRIZE-WINNING PIES & CAKES

CLASSIC TARTS

butter tarts

rustic fruit tarts

CLASSIC CAKES

purple plum upside-down
cake

carrot cake with cream
cheese icing

double-double chocolate cake
with chocolate icing

vanilla bean cheesecake

walnut torte

strawberries & cream roll

favourite pie crust

A great pie starts with a great pie crust. In researching this section of the cookbook, we spoke to dozens of beribboned bakers. The ingredients they used in their crusts were all similar, except when it came to the fat used: all butter, all vegetable shortening, all lard, part butter and part shortening, etc. So, we decided to take what we'd learned and conduct some baking tests. The result? Our favourite crust, by far, was made from lard and butter. It was flaky, tender, buttery, and golden brown. Makes 2 discs of pastry: enough for one 9-inch (23 cm) double-crust pie or two 9-inch (23 cm) single-crust pies.

2¼ cups (560 mL) all-purpose flour
1 tsp (5 mL) fine sea salt
½ cup (125 mL) lard, cubed
½ cup (125 mL) cold unsalted
    butter, cubed
1 large egg
2 tsp (10 mL) white vinegar
Ice cold water

Sift together the flour and salt in a large bowl. Incorporate the lard and butter using a pastry cutter or a food processor. The crumbs should be the size of peas.

Beat the egg and vinegar together in a liquid measuring cup. Add enough ice cold water to equal ½ cup (125 mL) of liquid. Pour the liquid over the dough. Knead, or pulse in the food processor, until the dough comes together in a ball. A little extra water may be required to incorporate all the flour.

Divide the dough into halves. Shape each half into a flat disc and wrap it in plastic wrap. Chill the dough for at least 1 hour prior to rolling.

STORAGE Any unused dough can be stored for up to 1 week in the refrigerator or frozen until needed.

If freezing, double wrap the dough in plastic wrap until ready to use. Defrost slowly in the refrigerator.

▶ The quality of the fat used in the pie crust is important. Rendered leaf lard can be difficult to find, but it's considered to be vastly superior to supermarket brands. (It's the type of lard our great-grandmothers would have used, rendered from the creamy white fat that surrounds the kidneys of a hog.) For the butter, seek out unsalted butter that contains more than 80 percent butterfat. The higher the butterfat content, the better the crust.

When working with the pie dough, be sure to use a gentle touch and do not overwork the dough.

ROLLING PIE DOUGH

Scatter a handful of flour onto a clean, flat work surface when ready to roll out 1 disc of the dough. (Any counter will work, but a marble surface is ideal.)

Roll the dough out from the centre to the outer edges using a rolling pin. (Avoid moving the pin backwards; rolling the dough out from the centre is best.) Roll the dough out as evenly and thinly as possible, without breaking or tearing it. The dough will be about ⅛ inch (3 mm) thick. Lift the dough frequently to prevent it from sticking, and use additional flour on the work surface and rolling pin, if needed. The completed round should be at least 3 inches (8 cm) wider than the diameter of the pie plate.

Fold the rolled dough in half, then lift and fit it into the pie plate. Pie plates come in all sorts of materials: metal, glass, ceramic. Each has a different impact on the resulting crust. We find that glass pie plates with wide rims tend to crisp and brown pie crusts evenly.

Follow pie recipe instructions.

apple pie

When we were teenagers, it never even occurred to us to enter baked goods in the Harrow Fair. But our friend Matt Ryan was always ahead of the crowd. Enticed by the $100 prize, he entered an apple pie back when he was only 14 years old. His winning recipe is below. The secrets to his success were revealed in a humorous article that appeared in the Windsor Star *back in 1985 (see sidebar).* Makes one 9-inch (23 cm) pie.

FILLING

8 cups (2 L) peeled, cored, and sliced apples
¾ cup (185 mL) granulated sugar
2 Tbsp (30 mL) all-purpose flour
½ tsp (2 mL) ground cinnamon
¼ tsp (1 mL) freshly grated nutmeg
½ tsp (2 mL) fine sea salt
2 Tbsp (30 mL) whipping cream
1 Tbsp (15 mL) unsalted butter, cubed

CRUST

1 recipe Favourite Pie Crust (page 156)
1 large egg
2 Tbsp (30 mL) milk
1 Tbsp (15 mL) granulated sugar

THE
HARROW
FAIR

1st

Preheat the oven to 450°F (230°C).

Roll out 1 disc of dough and fit it into a 9-inch (23 cm) deep-dish pie plate, trimming to ½ inch (1 cm) past the edge of the pie plate.

Combine the apples, sugar, flour, cinnamon, nutmeg, and salt in a large bowl. Spoon the filling into the pie shell, spreading evenly. Drizzle the cream over the apple mixture and dot the apples with the butter.

Roll out the second disc of dough. Lay the top crust over the pie filling and trim a ½ inch (1 cm) overhang. Tuck the overhang under the bottom crust border and crimp the two together to seal.

Whisk the egg and milk together in a small bowl. Brush the top crust with the egg wash, then sprinkle with sugar. Cut a pattern of holes in the top crust to let the steam escape.

Bake for 15 minutes, then reduce the heat to 350°F (180°C) and bake for an additional 50 minutes, or until the filling is bubbling and the crust is golden brown.

Cool to room temperature before serving.

STORAGE Fruit pies can be covered with aluminum foil and stored at room temperature for up to 2 days.

FROM THE *WINDSOR STAR*, 1985

"Last week marked the opening of the Harrow Fair and the apple pie judging was one of the main events. Matthew Ryan of Centre Street, Harrow, came away with 1st prize. Matthew is 14 years old and his pie was voted the best out of 27 entries. It may seem odd that a 14-year-old boy would spend his time baking pies, but the $100 1st prize offered by Murray's Orchards was enough to draw him into the contest.

"According to Matthew, this is the fifth pie he has made. He says he realized he was up against farm wives who have made so many apple pies they have lost count, but he credits natural talent for the win.

"Matthew was willing to share his award-winning filling recipe with us but he would not give away the secret crust mixture. That, he says, is a specialty he learned from his mom and she wouldn't want it spread around."

peaches & cream pie

This pie has won several 1st prize ribbons for Helen Klomp over the years. It has also raised thousands of dollars for charity, so it's surely one of the all-time best pies of the Harrow Fair. It took a bit of coaxing, but Helen eventually agreed to share her absolutely delicious recipe. Lucky us! Makes one 9-inch (23 cm) pie.

FILLING

¼ cup (60 mL) granulated sugar
1 Tbsp (15 mL) quick-cooking tapioca
Pinch fine sea salt
1 cup (250 mL) whipping cream
¼ tsp (1 mL) pure vanilla extract
4 cups (1 L) peeled, pitted, and sliced
    fresh peaches

CRUST

1 recipe Favourite Pie Crust (page 156)
2 Tbsp (30 mL) whipping cream
1 Tbsp (15 mL) granulated sugar

THE
HARROW
FAIR

1st

Preheat the oven to 375°F (190°C).

Whisk together the sugar, tapioca, and salt in a large bowl. Whisk in the cream and vanilla until combined. Gently toss the peaches in the cream mixture. Set aside for 15 minutes at room temperature.

Roll out 1 disc of pie crust and fit it into a 9-inch (23 cm) deep-dish pie plate, trimming the pastry to ½ inch (1 cm) past the edge of the pie plate. Spoon the filling into the pie shell.

Apply a lattice top crust (page 162). Brush the lattice with cream, then sprinkle with sugar.

Bake for 55 minutes or until the filling is bubbling and the crust is golden brown.

Cool to room temperature before serving.

STORAGE   This pie can be covered in plastic wrap and stored in the refrigerator for up to 2 days.

▶ When it comes to baking pies, there are a few tricks the best pie makers tend to use:
- Bake the pie in a deep-dish pie plate made of glass, preferably one with a wide rim.
- Place the pie on a metal baking sheet that has been placed in the oven before preheating. The metal baking sheet will catch any drips and will help form a crisp bottom crust. It might also speed up the cooking time by a few minutes, so be sure to check on your pie as it nears its estimated completion time.
- Bake the pie on the oven's middle rack.

MAKING A LATTICE TOP CRUST

Roll out 1 disc of pie crust. Using a sharp knife and a ruler as a guide, cut the dough into 1-inch (2.5 cm) strips. Some strips will be longer than others, but this is appropriate, as different lengths are needed to make the lattice.

Starting with the 2 longest strips, lay them perpendicular to each other on the pie filling already placed in the pie shell, forming an X in the centre of the pie. Working outward, alternate laying down horizontal strips and vertical strips, weaving them in an over-and-under basket-weave pattern as you go. Use the shortest strips for the outer edges of the lattice.

There should be open squares visible between the dough strips. This allows the filling to release steam while it is baking, and it also creates a beautiful pie.

rhubarb custard pie

A 1st prize winner for Lori, this is one of our family's favourite pies. The original recipe came from our Grandma McDonald. The combination of sweet custard and tart rhubarb is divine. Makes one 9-inch (23 cm) pie.

FILLING
1½ cups (375 mL) granulated sugar
¼ cup (60 mL) all-purpose flour
¾ tsp (4 mL) freshly grated nutmeg
¼ tsp (1 mL) fine sea salt
3 large eggs, beaten
4 cups (1 L) sliced fresh rhubarb
    (½-inch/1 cm pieces)
2 Tbsp (30 mL) unsalted butter

CRUST
1 recipe Favourite Pie Crust (page 156)
1 large egg
2 Tbsp (30 mL) milk
1 Tbsp (15 mL) granulated sugar

THE HARROW FAIR

1st

Preheat the oven to 375°F (190°C).

Combine the sugar, flour, nutmeg, and salt in a large bowl. Add the eggs and mix well. Stir in the rhubarb and mix well.

Roll out one disc of pie crust and fit it into a 9-inch (23 cm) deep-dish pie plate, trimming the pastry to ½ inch (1 cm) past the edge of the pie plate. Spoon the filling into the pie shell.

Dot the filling with butter. Apply a lattice top crust (page 162). Whisk together the egg and milk. Brush the lattice with the egg wash, then sprinkle with sugar.

Bake for 30 minutes. Reduce the heat to 325°F (160°C). Bake for an additional 45 minutes or until the custard is set and the crust is golden brown. A toothpick inserted into the centre of the pie will be slightly sticky when removed, but the custard should look set.

Cool to room temperature before serving.

STORAGE This pie can be covered in plastic wrap and stored in the refrigerator for up to 2 days.

▸ Rhubarb seems to be a fixture in many backyards in the area and it's readily available at local farm stands.

Rhubarb is one of the first plants to be ready for harvest in the spring, usually in late April or early May. It is at its most tender and flavourful at this time, although it continues to grow throughout the summer.

Freshly cut stalks are firm and glossy. Choose red ones for the colour they will add to this pie.

▸ More than 900 homemade pies are sold in the Harrow Fair Pie Tent every year. Local volunteers assemble the pies when the various fruits are in season throughout the year. The unbaked pies are then frozen, to be baked off throughout the Labour Day weekend. Pie varieties include apple, strawberry, rhubarb, strawberry-rhubarb, blueberry, raisin, peach, peach-blueberry, cherry, and elderberry.

pumpkin pie

This is the first pie Moira ever entered in the Harrow Fair. It won a ribbon in the World-Class Pumpkin Pie Contest and she was hooked. Serve with a generous dollop of whipped cream (page 171). Makes one 9-inch (23 cm) pie.

FILLING

¾ cup (185 mL) firmly packed brown sugar
½ tsp (2 mL) fine sea salt
1 tsp (5 mL) ground cinnamon
½ tsp (2 mL) ground mace
2 large eggs, beaten
1¾ cups (435 mL) pumpkin purée (see note)
¾ cup (185 mL) coconut milk
¼ cup (60 mL) whipping cream

CRUST

1 disc Favourite Pie Crust (page 156)

Preheat the oven to 450°F (230°C).

Combine the sugar, salt, cinnamon, and mace in a large mixing bowl. Stir in the eggs. Add the pumpkin, making sure that the mixture is well blended.

Stir in the coconut milk and whipping cream.

Roll out 1 disc of the pie crust and use it to line a 9-inch (23 cm) pie plate. Trim and crimp the edge as desired. Pour the filling into the pie crust.

Bake for 20 minutes. Reduce the heat to 350°F (180°C). Bake for an additional 30 minutes or until the filling is slightly firm and the crust is golden brown.

Cool to room temperature before serving with whipped cream (page 171).

STORAGE   This pie can be covered in plastic wrap and stored in the refrigerator for up to 2 days.

▶ SUGAR PUMPKIN PURÉE   For years, we shied away from making our own pumpkin purée, believing it was too much work. But it's really simple and makes the final result worth the effort.

When buying sugar pumpkins, seek out pumpkins that seem heavy for their size. They have a high moisture content and will yield a much silkier pumpkin purée.

Preheat the oven to 375°F (190°C). Cut a medium-sized sugar pumpkin in half. Place the halves, seed side up, on a baking sheet and cover with aluminum foil. Bake for 45 minutes. Turn the pumpkins over and continue cooking for 45 minutes or until a fork easily pierces the pumpkin flesh.

When the pumpkins have cooled enough to handle, clean out the seeds and peel the skin off with a paring knife. Transfer the flesh to a food processor and purée until smooth. Store in the refrigerator for up to 1 week or freeze for up to 6 months.

raspberry & cherry pie

With the bounty of an entire orchard at her disposal, is it any wonder that Leslie Balsillie is a ringer when it comes to winning red ribbons? Leslie and her husband, Doug, own The Fruit Wagon, which sells their produce throughout the spring, summer, and fall. This is Leslie's 1st prize–winning Raspberry & Cherry Pie recipe. Makes one 9-inch (23 cm) pie.

FILLING

3 cups (750 mL) fresh raspberries
3 cups (750 mL) pitted fresh sour cherries
1 cup (250 mL) granulated sugar
¼ cup (60 mL) cornstarch
2 Tbsp (30 mL) water

CRUST

1 recipe Favourite Pie Crust (page 156)
1 Tbsp (15 mL) granulated sugar
¼ tsp (1 mL) ground cinnamon

THE HARROW FAIR

1st

Stir together the raspberries, sour cherries, and sugar in a large saucepan. Cook over medium heat until the sugar is dissolved and the juice starts to bubble.

In a small bowl, combine the cornstarch with the water and mix until smooth. Add the cornstarch and water to the hot fruit and cook for 3 minutes or until thick. Cool the mixture before filling the pie crust.

Preheat the oven to 450°F (230°C).

Roll out 1 disc of dough and fit into a 9-inch (23 cm) deep-dish pie plate, trimming the pastry to ½ inch (1 cm) past the edge of the pie plate. Spoon the filling into the pie shell, spreading evenly.

Apply a lattice top crust (see page 162).

Combine the sugar and cinnamon in a small bowl and sprinkle the top of the pie. Bake for 15 minutes. Reduce the heat to 350°F (180°C), and bake for an additional 45 minutes or until the filling is bubbling and the crust is golden brown.

Cool to room temperature before serving.

STORAGE This pie can be covered in aluminum foil and stored at room temperature for up to 2 days.

wild black raspberry & blueberry pie

Gayle Hedges is a bit of a legend at the Harrow Fair. She's been entering items into the baked goods contests for more than 50 years, and she holds the record for having raised the most money at the Pie Auction. A whopping $2,400 was donated to charity in exchange for her Wild Black Raspberry & Blueberry Pie. Makes one 9-inch (23 cm) pie.

FILLING

3 cups (750 mL) wild fresh black
    raspberries
1 cup (250 mL) fresh blueberries
1 cup (250 mL) granulated sugar
2 Tbsp (30 mL) all-purpose flour
2 Tbsp (30 mL) fresh lemon juice
⅛ tsp (0.5 mL) fine sea salt
1 Tbsp (15 mL) unsalted butter

CRUST

1 recipe Favourite Pie Crust (page 156)
1 large egg
2 Tbsp (30 mL) milk
1 Tbsp (15 mL) granulated sugar

Stir together the berries, sugar, and flour in a large saucepan. Cook over medium heat for 5 minutes or until thick. Remove the pan from the heat and stir in the lemon juice, salt, and butter. Cool the mixture before filling the pie crust.

Preheat the oven to 450°F (230°C).

Roll out a disc of pie dough and fit it into a 9-inch (23 cm) deep-dish pie plate, trimming the pastry to ½ inch (1 cm) past the edge of the pie plate. Spoon the filling into the pie shell, spreading evenly.

Roll out a second disc of dough. Cover the pie. Trim and crimp the edges together, as desired. Whisk the egg and milk together in a small bowl. Brush the top crust with the egg wash, then sprinkle with sugar. Cut a pattern of holes in the top crust to let the steam escape.

Bake for 10 minutes. Reduce the heat to 350°F (180°C), and bake for an additional 35 minutes or until the filling is bubbling and the crust is golden brown.

Cool to room temperature before serving.

STORAGE This pie can be covered in aluminum foil and stored at room temperature for up to 2 days.

▶ Gayle has a secret spot in Harrow where she picks her wild black raspberries. If you're not lucky enough to have your own source for wild raspberries, cultivated black raspberries from a farm stand will make a fine substitute.

▶ When baking pies, if the edges of the crust start to become too dark before the filling is cooked and bubbling, cut out strips of aluminum foil, 2 inches (5 cm) wide, and fasten them around the edge of the pie. Continue to bake until fully cooked.

cream pie

As tempting as it is to throw this pie in someone's face, we urge you to control yourself and eat a slice instead. Makes one 9-inch (23 cm) pie.

FILLING

¾ cup (185 mL) granulated sugar
¼ tsp (1 mL) fine sea salt
3 cups (750 mL) milk
3 large egg yolks
3 Tbsp (45 mL) cornstarch
1½ Tbsp (22 mL) all-purpose flour
1½ Tbsp (22 mL) unsalted butter
1 Tbsp (15 mL) pure vanilla extract

CRUST

1 disc Favourite Pie Crust (page 156)

Whipped cream (facing page)

CRUST

Preheat the oven to 375°F (190°C).

Roll out a disc of pie crust and fit it into a 9-inch (23 cm) pie plate. Trim and crimp the edge as desired.

Line the crust with a large piece of aluminum foil or parchment paper. Fill with pie weights or dry beans to weigh the crust down as it is baking.

Bake for 15 minutes. Remove the weights and foil. Bake for another 10 minutes or until the crust is golden brown. If the crust puffs up, gently push it back down into place. Remove from the oven and cool completely before filling.

FILLING

Whisk together the sugar, salt, and milk in a large saucepan. Cook over medium heat, stirring constantly, until the mixture comes to a boil. Boil for 2 minutes. Remove the pan from the heat.

Stir together the egg yolks, cornstarch, and flour in a medium-sized bowl. Whisk in 1 Tbsp (15 mL) of the hot mixture, stirring vigorously. Add another spoonful, then mix the egg yolk mixture into the milk mixture. Place the pan over medium-low heat for another 2 minutes, stirring constantly until the mixture starts to thicken. Remove from the heat. Stir in the butter and vanilla. Cool to room temperature.

Pour the cooled filling into the cooled pie shell, spreading evenly. Place a piece of plastic wrap directly on the filling and refrigerate for at least 1 hour.

Cover the top of the pie with whipped cream (facing page) and serve immediately.

STORAGE   If you're planning on serving only a few slices of cream pie, top each slice individually with whipped cream. Whipped cream should top the whole pie only if it's going to be enjoyed all at once.

This cream pie can be covered in plastic wrap and placed in the refrigerator for up to 2 days.

whipped cream

Our dad, Chuck McDonald, becomes irked (some might say distraught) when served a slice of home-made pie without fresh whipped cream. It's one of the few things that make him lose his sense of humour.

Makes 4 cups (1 L).

2 cups (500 mL) cold whipping cream
2 Tbsp (30 mL) granulated sugar

Place the metal whisk attachment and metal bowl of a stand mixer in a freezer for at least 15 minutes. Remove once cold and assemble the mixer as usual.

Whip the cream on medium-high speed until it starts to thicken. Add the sugar and whip until soft peaks are formed.

Use immediately. (Whipped cream is best made at the last minute, not in advance.)

raisin pie

When one of Pat Fitzpatrick's pies is up for grabs in the Pie Auction, hands shoot into the air to place bids. This recipe, for Pat's famous raisin pie, is just one of her many 1st prize winners. Makes one 9-inch (23 cm) pie.

FILLING

1 cup (250 mL) firmly packed
    brown sugar
2 Tbsp (30 mL) cornstarch
2 cups (500 mL) raisins
1 cup (250 mL) water
½ cup (125 mL) fresh orange juice
2 Tbsp (30 mL) fresh lemon juice
½ tsp (2 mL) orange zest
½ tsp (2 mL) lemon zest
½ cup (125 mL) chopped toasted wal-
    nuts (see note on page 222)

CRUST

1 recipe Favourite Pie Crust (page 156)
1 Tbsp (15 mL) whipping cream
1 Tbsp (15 mL) granulated sugar

THE
HARROW
FAIR

1st

Mix together the sugar, cornstarch, raisins, water, orange juice, lemon juice, and zests in a large saucepan set over medium heat. Stir frequently, until the mixture is thick and bubbly. Cook for 1 additional minute. Remove from the heat and stir in the walnuts. Cool the mixture before filling the pie crust.

Preheat the oven to 375°F (190°C).

Roll out 1 disc of pie crust and use it to line a 9-inch (23 cm) deep-dish pie plate, trimming the pastry to ½ inch (1 cm) past the edge of the pie plate. Spoon the filling into the pie shell, spreading evenly.

Apply a lattice top crust (see page 162). Trim and crimp the edge as desired. Brush with cream, then sprinkle with sugar.

Bake for 45 minutes or until the filling is bubbling and the crust is golden brown.

Serve warm.

STORAGE   This pie can be covered in aluminum foil and stored at room temperature for up to 2 days.

▶ The Pie Auction at the Harrow Fair is an event not to be missed. Here's how it works . . .

When pies are dropped off for judging on the Wednesday before Labour Day Weekend, entrants are asked if they would like their pie to be auctioned off. If yes, the pie goes through the judging process on Thursday and is then taken to the main stage for the live auction.

A large crowd gathers on the hay bale benches in front of the stage. At 6 p.m., the bidding begins. The two auctioneers promote the merits of each pie to the crowd—the type of pie, who baked it, and any ribbons it won. Each year, more than 100 pies are auctioned off and thousands of dollars are raised for the John McGivney Children's Centre, a charity benefiting children and families in Essex County and Windsor.

The pie auction gets more popular every year. It's a fun event that benefits a great cause.

butter tarts

One year, Moira was intent upon winning a ribbon for her butter tarts. She decided to stack the deck, and entered two different recipes into the category. But her efforts were unrewarded—she lost to the very talented Francy Pearman. Francy's butter tarts are fabulous and well-deserving of the 1st prize ribbon. Makes twelve 2-inch (5 cm) tarts.

FILLING

⅓ cup (80 mL) unsalted butter,
 melted
1 cup (250 mL) firmly packed
 brown sugar
2 Tbsp (30 mL) milk
1 large egg, beaten
1 tsp (5 mL) pure vanilla extract
⅓ cup (80 mL) currants

CRUST

1 disc Favourite Pie Crust (page 156)

Preheat the oven to 450°F (230°C). Lightly grease a 12-cup muffin pan.

Roll out the pie crust. Cut twelve 5-inch (12 cm) rounds out of the pie crust. Fit each round into the muffin pan, making 12 tart shells.

Mix together the melted butter, sugar, milk, egg, and vanilla in a large bowl.

Place a little over 1 tsp (5 mL) dried currants in each tart shell. Add approximately 2 Tbsp (30 mL) of the filling mixture to each tart shell.

Bake for 8 minutes. Reduce the temperature to 350°F (180°C). Bake for an additional 15 minutes or until the tart shells are golden brown. Cool for 5 minutes, then transfer the tarts to a rack.

Cool to room temperature before serving.

STORAGE Store the tarts in an airtight container in the refrigerator for up to 1 week.

rustic fruit tarts

These tarts are made by folding the edges of the pie dough over the top of the ripe fruit filling, creating a rustic, free-form look. Simple and delicious—it's the perfect dessert to serve to guests. Makes four 4-inch (10 cm) tarts.

CRUST

1 disc Favourite Pie Crust (page 156)
1 Tbsp (15 mL) milk
1 Tbsp (15 mL) granulated sugar

BLACKBERRY FILLING

3 cups (750 mL) fresh blackberries
½ cup (125 mL) granulated sugar
1 Tbsp (15 mL) fresh lemon juice
1 Tbsp (15 mL) cornstarch

PEAR FILLING

3 cups (750 mL) thinly sliced
   fresh pears
½ cup (125 mL) granulated sugar
1 Tbsp (15 mL) fresh lemon juice
1 Tbsp (15 mL) cornstarch
¼ tsp (1 mL) ground cinnamon

PLUM FILLING

3 cups (750 mL) quartered fresh
   Italian plums
½ cup (125 mL) granulated sugar
1 Tbsp (15 mL) fresh lemon juice
1 Tbsp (15 mL) cornstarch
¼ tsp (1 mL) ground cardamom

APRICOT FILLING

3 cups (750 mL) quartered fresh
   apricots
½ cup (125 mL) granulated sugar
1 Tbsp (15 mL) fresh lemon juice
1 Tbsp (15 mL) cornstarch
1 tsp (5 mL) pure vanilla extract

Preheat the oven to 350°F (180°C). Line a large baking sheet with parchment paper.

Divide 1 disc of pie crust into quarters. Shape each quarter into a smaller disc. Roll each disc into a 6-inch (15 cm) round. Place each round of pastry on the baking sheet.

Mix the filling ingredients together in a medium-sized bowl. Dividing it evenly 4 ways, heap the filling in the centre of each round. Fold the edges of the crust up toward the middle, leaving a 2-inch (5 cm) opening in the centre of the tart for the filling to peek through.

Brush the crusts with milk and sprinkle with sugar.

Bake for 25 minutes or until the filling is bubbling and the crust is golden brown.

Cool the tarts to room temperature before serving.

STORAGE These tarts can be covered in aluminum foil and stored at room temperature for up to 2 days.

purple plum upside-down cake

This cake recipe made its debut in the "Any Fruit Upside-Down Cake" category at the Harrow Fair. It turned out beautifully and we were sure that out of all our entries it was the most ribbon-worthy. Then it was disqualified for being incorrectly cut. We won't make the same mistake twice! Makes one 10-inch (25 cm) round cake.

¾ cup (185 mL) unsalted butter, softened, divided
¾ cup (185 mL) firmly packed brown sugar
8 Italian purple plums, halved
1¼ cups (310 mL) all-purpose flour
1 tsp (5 mL) baking powder
½ tsp (2 mL) baking soda
¼ tsp (1 mL) fine sea salt
⅔ cup (160 mL) granulated sugar
3 large eggs
1 tsp (5 mL) pure vanilla extract
½ cup (125 mL) sour cream

Melt ¼ cup (60 mL) of the butter in a 10-inch (25 cm) cast iron skillet set over medium heat. Stir in the brown sugar until it is bubbling. Spread the sugar mixture evenly around the bottom of the pan, then remove the pan from the heat.

Starting from the outside, place the plum halves in the pan, cut side up. Do not overcrowd the pan.

Preheat the oven to 375°F (190°C).

Sift together the flour, baking powder, baking soda, and salt in a medium-sized bowl.

Cream the remaining ½ cup (125 mL) softened butter with the granulated sugar in the bowl of a stand mixer fitted with the paddle attachment. Beat in the eggs one at a time. Beat in the vanilla.

Beat the dry ingredients into the wet ingredients, alternating with the sour cream. Beat until just combined. Pour the batter over the plums set in the skillet, spreading evenly.

Bake for 40 minutes or until a toothpick inserted into the centre of the cake comes out clean.

Rest the cake for 5 minutes, then invert the skillet onto a large serving plate. (Do not wait any longer than 5 minutes or the cake will stick to the skillet.)

Serve warm.

▶ Italian purple plums are locally available from late August through September.

▶ A well-seasoned cast iron skillet is essential for making this cake. To season a new pan or revive a neglected one, wash the pan in warm, soapy water. Dry completely and coat the inside with vegetable oil. Leave in a 300°F (150°C) oven for 1 hour. Turn off the heat and leave the pan in the oven to cool. Wipe any remaining oil out of the pan before using. To keep your skillet in good shape, don't use dish soap and scrub the surface gently.

carrot cake

Since being bitten by the ribbon bug, we have become a bit evangelical about persuading friends and family to enter the baking competitions. Our friend Janette Lawton took up the challenge, and won 1st prize for her carrot cake. When you make it, you'll know why. Makes one 9- × 13-inch (23 × 33 cm) cake.

2 cups (500 mL) all-purpose flour
2 tsp (10 mL) baking powder
1½ tsp (7 mL) baking soda
½ tsp (2 mL) fine sea salt
2 tsp (10 mL) ground cinnamon
4 large eggs
2 cups (500 mL) granulated sugar
1 cup (250 mL) vegetable oil
½ cup (125 mL) applesauce (page 9)
1 cup (250 mL) finely chopped toasted
    pecans (see note on page 222)
2 cups (500 mL) grated carrots
1½ cups (375 mL) drained crushed
    pineapple

Preheat the oven to 350°F (180°C). Butter a 9- × 13-inch (23 × 33 cm) baking pan or butter the sides and line the bottom with parchment paper.

Sift together the flour, baking powder, baking soda, salt, and cinnamon in a large bowl. Beat the eggs, sugar, oil, and applesauce together in the bowl of a stand mixer fitted with the paddle attachment.

Beat the dry ingredients into the wet ingredients, until just combined. Gently fold in the pecans, grated carrots, and pineapple.

Pour the batter into the prepared pan, spreading evenly.

Bake for 45 minutes or until a toothpick inserted into the centre of the cake comes out clean.

Cool to room temperature before covering with cream cheese icing.

cream cheese icing

½ cup (125 mL) cream cheese,
    softened
¼ cup (60 mL) unsalted butter,
    softened
½ tsp (2 mL) pure vanilla extract
2 cups (500 mL) sifted icing sugar

Cream together the cream cheese and butter until light and smooth, in the bowl of a stand mixer fitted with the paddle attachment. Add the vanilla and the icing sugar. Mix until the icing is very smooth and glossy.

THE
HARROW
FAIR

1st

double-double chocolate cake

Double chocolate. Double layer. And a cupful of "double-double": Canada's most popular preparation of Tim Hortons coffee, boasting double the cream, double the sugar. This recipe makes a fabulous cake that's worthy of the double ribbons Moira won at the Harrow Fair. Makes one 8-inch (20 cm) round layer cake.

2 oz (60 g) bittersweet chocolate, chopped (see note on page 191)
2 cups (500 mL) all-purpose flour
1¼ cups (310 mL) granulated sugar
½ cup (125 mL) cocoa powder
2 tsp (10 mL) baking soda
1 tsp (5 mL) baking powder
1 tsp (5 mL) fine sea salt
1 cup (250 mL) buttermilk (see note on page 49)
½ cup (125 mL) vegetable oil
2 large eggs
1 tsp (5 mL) pure vanilla extract
1 cup (250 mL) double-double coffee

Melt the chocolate in a double boiler or a small saucepan set on low heat. Stir constantly until the mixture is smooth. Set aside to cool.

Preheat the oven to 350°F (180°C). Butter and flour two 8-inch (20 cm) round cake pans.

Sift together the flour, sugar, cocoa, baking soda, baking powder, and salt in a large bowl. Mix together the buttermilk, oil, eggs, and vanilla in the bowl of a stand mixer fitted with the paddle attachment.

Add the dry ingredients to the wet ingredients with the mixer on low speed. Add the melted chocolate and the double-double coffee and mix just until combined. Pour the batter into the pans, spreading evenly.

Bake for 35 minutes or until a toothpick inserted into the centre of a cake comes out clean.

Cool the cakes in the pans until they are easy to handle.

chocolate icing

2 oz (60 g) bittersweet chocolate, chopped (see note on page 191)
1 cup (250 mL) unsalted butter, softened
2 cups (500 mL) sifted icing sugar
¼ cup (60 mL) whipping cream

Melt the chocolate in a double boiler or a small saucepan set on low heat. Stir constantly until the mixture is smooth. Set aside to cool.

Whip the butter in the bowl of a stand mixer fitted with the whisk attachment. Add the melted and cooled chocolate and mix until combined.

Slowly add the icing sugar to the chocolate mixture. Add the whipping cream. Continue mixing until the icing is smooth and thoroughly combined.

Whisk on high for 1 minute more or until the icing is smooth and spreadable.

ASSEMBLY
Invert a cake onto a cake platter. Spread the top with chocolate icing. Place the second cake on top of the icing. Spread the remaining icing evenly over the top and sides of the cake.

vanilla bean cheesecake

A homemade shortbread-pecan crust holds up a vanilla-flecked, cream cheese filling. Serve with Over-the-Top Cherry Sauce (page 11). Makes one 10-inch (20 cm) round cheesecake.

CRUST

2 cups (500 mL) shortbread cookie crumbs (page 204)
½ cup (125 mL) finely ground toasted pecans (see note on page 222)
½ tsp (2 mL) ground cinnamon

FILLING

1 lb (500 g) cream cheese, softened
1 lb (500 g) ricotta cheese
1½ cups (375 mL) granulated sugar
2 Tbsp (30 mL) cornstarch
4 large eggs, at room temperature
2 tsp (10 mL) pure vanilla extract
Seeds scraped from 1 vanilla bean
2 cups (500 mL) sour cream

CRUST

Preheat the oven to 425°F (220°C). Prepare a 10-inch (3 L) springform pan by lining the bottom and the sides with parchment paper. Anchor the paper with small dots of butter.

Mix together the shortbread cookie crumbs, pecans, and cinnamon in a medium-sized bowl. Press the mixture into the bottom of the prepared pan.

Bake the crust for 5 minutes.

FILLING

Mix together the cream cheese and ricotta until fluffy in the bowl of a stand mixer fitted with the paddle attachment.

Mix together the sugar and cornstarch in a separate bowl, then stir into the cheese mixture. Blend until smooth. Add the eggs, one at a time, beating well after each addition. Stir in the vanilla extract, vanilla bean seeds, and sour cream until just combined.

Pour the filling into the prepared crust. Place the cheesecake on a rack in the middle of the oven.

Bake for 15 minutes at 425°F (220°C). Lower the oven to 300°F (150°C) and bake for an additional 1 hour or until the cake is largely set but the middle still wiggles slightly.

Remove the cheesecake from the oven and let it cool completely on a rack. Cover and refrigerate until ready to eat, at least 2 hours.

STORAGE Keep covered in the refrigerator for up to 1 week.

▶ The best way to keep shelled nuts fresh is to keep them in the freezer.

walnut torte

This 1st prize–winning cake recipe is from Rose McLean. Layers of walnut cake are filled with a silky chocolate cream. In a word, scrumptious! Makes one 8-inch (20 cm) round layer cake.

BATTER

¼ cup (60 mL) bread crumbs
(page 137)
1 Tbsp (15 mL) rum (or lemon juice)
3½ cups (875 mL) finely ground toasted walnuts (see note on page 222)
2 Tbsp (30 mL) all-purpose flour
½ tsp (2 mL) baking powder
10 large eggs, separated
1 cup (250 mL) granulated sugar
⅛ tsp (0.5 mL) cream of tartar

FILLING

1 cup (250 mL) milk
3 Tbsp (45 mL) cornstarch
3 oz (90 g) bittersweet chocolate,
chopped (see note on page 191)
1 cup (250 mL) unsalted butter,
softened
1½ cups (375 mL) sifted icing sugar
1 egg yolk
1 Tbsp (15 mL) rum (or lemon juice)

THE HARROW FAIR

1st

Preheat the oven to 350°F (180°C). Butter two 8-inch (20 cm) round cake pans. Line the bottoms with parchment paper and then butter the paper.

Stir together the bread crumbs and rum in a small bowl and set aside for a few minutes to soak. Combine the walnuts, flour, and baking powder in a medium-sized bowl. Add the bread crumb mixture to the walnut mixture.

In the bowl of a stand mixer fitted with the paddle attachment, beat the 10 egg yolks and the sugar together until fluffy and lemon coloured, about 3 minutes. Turn the mixture into a separate large bowl.

Clean the bowl of the stand mixer thoroughly. Add the 10 egg whites. Beat using the whisk attachment until they double in volume. Add the cream of tartar and beat until the whites form stiff peaks, about 3 minutes.

Gently fold the walnut mixture into the egg yolk mixture, alternating with the egg whites and beginning and ending with the walnut mixture. Mix until just combined.

Pour the batter into the cake pans, spreading evenly. Bake for 30 minutes or until lightly golden.

Invert the cakes onto racks to cool to room temperature.

FILLING

While the cake is baking, whisk the milk and cornstarch together in a small saucepan until smooth. Add the chocolate.

Melt the mixture over low heat and cook, stirring constantly, until thick. Set the mixture aside to cool completely.

In the bowl of a stand mixer fitted with the paddle attachment, cream the butter, icing sugar, and egg yolk together until fluffy. Add the cooled chocolate mixture ½ cup (125 mL) at a time. Add the rum. Beat for another 10 minutes, until smooth.

ASSEMBLY

Cut the cooled cake layers in half horizontally, creating 4 layers.

On a cake plate, layer the cake layers with filling. Frost the top and sides of the cake with the remaining filling.

Refrigerate until ready to serve.

▶ This cake is good to serve the day it's made, but it's exceptionally good the day after, when its flavours have had a chance to mingle.

strawberries & cream roll

Our cousin Beth's birthday falls in the middle of our local strawberry season. The Straw-berries & Cream Roll—a light sponge cake rolled around fresh strawberries and whipped cream—is what her mom used to make for her every year. It's still her favourite. Makes 1 great birthday cake!

CAKE
1 cup (250 mL) all-purpose flour
1 tsp (5 mL) baking powder
¼ tsp (1 mL) fine sea salt
3 large eggs
1 cup (250 mL) granulated sugar
⅓ cup (80 mL) water
1 tsp (5 mL) pure vanilla extract
½ cup (125 mL) icing sugar (for kitchen towel)

FILLING
3 cups (750 mL) diced fresh strawberries
2 Tbsp (30 mL) granulated sugar
Whipped cream (using 2 cups/ 500 mL whipping cream, page 171)
¼ cup (60 mL) icing sugar

GARNISH
Fresh strawberries

Preheat the oven to 375°F (190°C). Line a 15- × 10- × 1-inch (38 × 25 × 2.5 cm) baking sheet with parchment paper.

Sift together the flour, baking powder, and salt in a medium-sized bowl.

Beat the eggs for 5 minutes at high speed in the bowl of a stand mixer fitted with the paddle attachment. Slowly add the sugar and beat for 1 minute. Beat in the water and vanilla until combined. Gradually add the dry ingredients, beating just until smooth.

Pour the batter onto the baking sheet, spreading evenly.

Bake for 12 minutes or until a toothpick inserted into the centre of the cake comes out clean.

While the cake is baking, sprinkle ½ cup (125 mL) icing sugar on a clean kitchen towel.

Remove the cake from the oven and loosen it from the edges of the pan. Cover the cake with the kitchen towel that has been sprinkled with icing sugar. Carefully invert the cake and towel onto a countertop. Remove the parchment paper and trim any dry edges, if necessary.

While the cake is still hot, carefully roll the cake in the towel, starting from a narrow end. Let the cake cool for at least 45 minutes on a baking rack.

While the cake is cooling, mix the strawberries with the 2 Tbsp (30 mL) granulated sugar. Set aside to macerate (soften by soaking).

Unroll the cake and remove the towel. Spread the whipped cream over the cake. Scatter the strawberries evenly on top of the whipped cream. Carefully re-roll the cake and place it on a large serving platter. Sprinkle with icing sugar.

Cut into thick slices. Garnish with fresh strawberries.

▶ If strawberries aren't in season, replace them with 1 cup (250 mL) strawberry jam. When assembling the cake, put the jam on the cake first, then add the whipped cream.

DUMPLINGS, COBBLERS, & CRISPS

apple dumplings

nectarine & blueberry cobbler

apple crisp

CLASSIC SQUARES

brownies

lemon squares

first date squares

raspberry squares

CLASSIC COOKIES

chocolate chip cookies

peanut butter cookies

sugar cookies with royal icing

gingersnaps

jam thumbprint cookies

shortbread cookies

SWEET
FAIR FARE

DOUGHNUTS

funnel cakes

jam doughnuts

apple fritter rings

ICY TREATS

frozen custard

melon creamsicles

grape snow

grape ice cream

mint chocolate ice cream

strawberry shortcake ice
  cream

ice cream sandwiches

SWEET STUFF

candy apples

salted peanut brittle

sponge toffee

maple caramel corn with nuts

apple dumplings

In 155 years of the Harrow Fair, Brenda Anger is the only woman to have been president of the Harrow Fair Board. She and her family have been involved in the organization of the fair for more than three decades. This is Brenda's recipe for apple dumplings. Whole apples are filled with butter, cinnamon, and sugar, then wrapped in a flaky pastry and basted with sweet syrup. They're divine. Makes 8 dumplings.

DUMPLINGS

2⅔ cups (660 mL) all-purpose flour
1 Tbsp (15 mL) baking powder
1½ tsp (7 mL) fine sea salt
1 cup + 8 tsp (250 mL + 40 mL) cold
    unsalted butter, cubed, divided
⅔ cup (160 mL) milk
8 medium Empire apples
1 tsp (5 mL) ground cinnamon
½ cup (125 mL) granulated sugar

SAUCE

1¼ cups (310 mL) firmly packed
    brown sugar
¾ cup (185 mL) water
½ cup (125 mL) unsalted butter

THE
HARROW
FAIR

authors'
FAVE

PASTRY

Sift together the flour, baking powder, and salt in a large bowl. Working quickly and with a light touch, incorporate the 1 cup (250 mL) butter with your fingers or a pastry cutter until the largest pieces are the size of peas. Stir in the milk. Toss the dough with a fork until it comes together. (Add a little more milk, if needed.)

Divide the dough into 8 pieces and shape into small discs.
Cover the discs with plastic wrap and refrigerate for 1 hour.

DUMPLINGS

Preheat the oven to 350°F (180°C). Butter a 9- × 13-inch (23 × 33 cm) baking pan.

Peel and core the apples, leaving each apple in one piece.

On a well-floured surface, roll each portion of dough into a 7-inch (18 cm) square. Place 1 apple on each square.

Mix the cinnamon and sugar together in a small bowl. Place 1 Tbsp (15 mL) of the cinnamon-sugar in the centre of each apple. Top each apple with 1 tsp (5 mL) of the 8 tsp (40 mL) butter.

For each apple, bring the 4 corners of pastry up to the top of the apple and pinch together to seal. Place the dumplings in the prepared pan.

Bake for 15 minutes while you make the basting sauce.

SAUCE

While the dumplings are baking, make the sauce by combining the brown sugar, water, and butter in a medium saucepan. Bring the ingredients to a boil, stirring often, over medium-high heat.

After the dumplings have been in the oven for 15 minutes, pour the sauce over the dumplings. Bake the dumplings for an additional 40 minutes. While dumplings are baking, spoon the sauce over the dumplings twice. (This gives the dumplings a shiny glaze and moistens the dough.)

Serve warm.

▶ The judges at the Harrow Fair evaluate 12 varieties of apples, ranging from the classic Red Delicious to newer varieties like Ginger Gold and Honeycrisp. The apples must come from the exhibitor's own holding and the stem must be attached to avoid disqualification.

nectarine & blueberry cobbler

Our mom likes making fruit cobblers to serve after dinner on Sundays in the summer. We've started the same tradition in our homes. Our Nectarine & Blueberry Cobbler is a great dessert for busy families because it's quick and easy to make. Serves 8.

4 cups (1 L) sliced fresh nectarines
1 cup (250 mL) fresh blueberries
¼ cup (60 mL) granulated sugar
1 Tbsp (15 mL) cornstarch
½ tsp (2 mL) lemon zest
2 cups (500 mL) all-purpose flour
¼ cup (60 mL) granulated sugar
1 Tbsp (15 mL) baking powder
½ tsp (2 mL) fine sea salt
6 Tbsp (90 mL) cold unsalted
    butter, cubed
¾ cup (185 mL) whipping cream

Preheat the oven to 350°F (180°C). Butter an 8-inch (20 cm) square baking dish.

Mix together the nectarines, blueberries, sugar, cornstarch, and lemon zest. Pour the fruit mixture into the prepared baking dish.

Sift together the flour, sugar, baking powder, and salt in a large bowl. Working quickly and with a light touch, incorporate the butter with your fingers or a pastry cutter until the largest pieces are the size of peas.

Pour the cream over the dry ingredients and mix with a fork until the dough comes together. Do not overwork the dough. The dough will be soft and sticky.

Spread the dough evenly across the fruit layer. A cobbler is meant to be rustic, so the topping shouldn't be smooth and perfect-looking. Poke several holes in the dough to allow the steam to escape while the cobbler is cooking.

Bake for 1 hour or until the top is puffed and golden brown. Serve warm.

STORAGE Cobblers don't improve with age. The whole cobbler should be enjoyed the day it's made.

▶ This cobbler can easily be made with other fruit combinations, such as these:
  • 4 cups (1 L) peaches + 1 cup (250 mL) blackberries
  • 3 cups (750 mL) sour cherries + 2 cups (500 mL) raspberries

apple crisp

Our best friends growing up were Shaila and Sarita Watsa, who lived within shouting distance of our house. This recipe is from their mother, Margaret. She's been making it the same way since we were kids, with good reason. Serves 8.

10 cups (2.5 L) peeled, cored, and
    sliced fresh apples
1 cup (250 mL) firmly packed
    brown sugar
¾ cup (185 mL) all-purpose flour
¾ cup (185 mL) old-fashioned
    rolled oats
½ tsp (2 mL) ground cloves
½ tsp (2 mL) ground cinnamon
½ tsp (2 mL) fine sea salt
½ cup (125 mL) unsalted butter,
    melted

Preheat the oven to 375°F (190°C). Butter a 9- × 13-inch (23 × 33 cm) baking pan.

Place the apple slices in the bottom of the baking pan.

Mix the sugar, flour, oats, cloves, cinnamon, and salt together in a large bowl. Stir in the melted butter, mixing thoroughly. Spread the crisp mixture on top of the apples.

Bake for 45 minutes, until the juices are bubbling and the crisp topping is golden brown.

Serve warm.

▶ In this recipe, we like experimenting with different local varietals of apples to see which work best. Lately we've been combining 5 cups (1.25 L) of a tart apple like Granny Smith with 5 cups (1.25 L) of a sweeter apple, like Braeburn or Golden Delicious. It gives this crisp a nice balance of flavours.

brownies

When evaluating baked goods at the Harrow Fair, judges look for perfectly perfect renditions of classic recipes. We worked on this recipe until we got it "just right." We can hardly wait to see what the judges think of these brownies next year. Makes 12 large brownies.

¾ cup (185 mL) unsalted butter
7 oz (200 g) bittersweet chocolate, chopped (see note)
4 large eggs
2 cups (500 mL) granulated sugar
2 tsp (10 mL) pure vanilla extract
1½ cups (375 mL) all-purpose flour
1 tsp (5 mL) fine sea salt

Preheat the oven to 325°F (160°C). Line a 9- × 13-inch (23 × 33 cm) baking pan with parchment paper that over-hangs the long sides of the pan by 1 inch (2.5 cm).

Melt the butter and chocolate in a double boiler or a small saucepan set on low heat. Stir constantly until the mixture is smooth. Set aside to cool.

Beat the eggs and sugar together in the bowl of a stand mixer fitted with the paddle attachment on high for 3 minutes or until light and fluffy. Add the vanilla and the cooled chocolate mixture. Beat on low speed until combined.

Sift together the flour and salt. Add the dry ingredients to the wet ingredients, beating on low speed until just combined. Pour the batter in the pan, spreading evenly.

Bake for 30 minutes or until the brownies appear to be set. The top will be crackled, and a toothpick inserted into the centre of the brownies will still be a bit sticky.

Cool the brownies to room temperature on a rack. Once cooled, invert the brownies onto a clean cutting board. Remove the parchment paper. Cut the brownies into 12 bars, about 3 inches (8 cm) square.

STORAGE   Store the brownies in an airtight container for up to 5 days.

▶ For best results, use the highest-quality bittersweet chocolate you can find. To ensure an intense chocolate flavour, it should have a cacao content of at least 60 percent.

When melting the chocolate, watch it closely. Dark chocolate has a tendency to burn faster than versions with a lower cacao content.

▶ Turn leftover brownies into a quick topping for ice cream. Place the brownies in the bowl of a food processor. Chop until the brownies are in crumbs. Place in a resealable plastic bag and store in the freezer until ready to sprinkle on ice cream.

lemon squares

There's no competitive category for lemon squares at the Harrow Fair. But this recipe, from Lori's mother-in-law, Roberta, is so good that we're considering lobbying the Fair Board to get a new category established. Makes 16 squares.

CRUST

1 cup (250 mL) all-purpose flour
¼ cup (60 mL) sifted icing sugar
½ cup (125 mL) unsalted butter, melted

FILLING

2 large eggs, beaten
1 cup (250 mL) granulated sugar
¼ cup (60 mL) fresh lemon juice
1 tsp (5 mL) lemon zest
2 Tbsp (30 mL) all-purpose flour
½ tsp (2 mL) baking powder
2 Tbsp (30 mL) sifted icing sugar

CRUST

Preheat the oven to 350°F (180°C).

Sift together the flour and icing sugar in a medium-sized bowl. Stir in the melted butter until well mixed. Press the crust into an 8-inch (20 cm) square baking pan.

Bake for 20 minutes or until the crust is lightly golden in colour.

FILLING

While the crust is baking, combine the eggs, sugar, lemon juice, and lemon zest in a medium-sized bowl. Mix well. Add the flour and baking powder and mix thoroughly.

Pour the filling on the crust, spreading evenly. Bake for 25 minutes or until the filling is set.

Cut the bars into 2-inch (5 cm) squares while they are still hot. Remove them from the pan and dust with icing sugar.

Cool to room temperature before serving.

STORAGE Store the squares in an airtight container in the refrigerator for up to 5 days.

first date squares

Moira's classic date square recipe won 1st prize at the Harrow Fair one year, earning itself a new name. Makes 16 squares.

CRUST

1½ cups (375 mL) old-fashioned rolled oats

1 cup (250 mL) all-purpose flour

½ tsp (2 mL) fine sea salt

½ cup (125 mL) unsalted butter, softened

¾ cup (185 mL) firmly packed brown sugar

FILLING

3 cups (750 mL) pitted dates

1 cup (250 mL) water

½ cup (125 mL) firmly packed brown sugar

1 Tbsp (15 mL) fresh lemon juice

1 tsp (5 mL) pure vanilla extract

CRUST

Preheat the oven to 350°F (180°C). Butter an 8-inch (20 cm) square baking pan or line the bottom and sides with parchment paper.

Combine the rolled oats, flour, and salt in a medium-sized bowl. Cream the butter and sugar in the bowl of a stand mixer fitted with the paddle attachment. Add the dry ingredients and blend until the mixture is thoroughly combined.

Press half the oatmeal mixture into the prepared pan.

FILLING

Combine the dates, water, brown sugar, and lemon juice in a medium-sized saucepan set over medium heat. Cook until the mixture becomes soft and thick, about 10 minutes. Add the vanilla.

Spread the filling evenly over the bottom crust. Sprinkle the remaining crust on top, pressing gently.

Bake for 25 minutes or until the top crust is golden brown.

Cool to room temperature before cutting.

STORAGE Store the squares in an airtight container in the refrigerator for up to 5 days.

raspberry squares

Our raspberry squares are simple and classic. And scrumptious. Makes 24 squares.

BASE

¾ cup (185 mL) unsalted butter,
  softened
½ cup (125 mL) granulated sugar
1½ cups (375 mL) all-purpose flour
½ tsp (2 mL) fine sea salt
1 cup (250 mL) raspberry jam (see
  note on page 6)

TOPPING

1 cup (250 mL) all-purpose flour
½ cup (125 mL) old-fashioned
  rolled oats
½ cup (125 mL) firmly packed
  brown sugar
½ tsp (2 mL) fine sea salt
½ cup (125 mL) unsalted butter,
  softened

BASE

Preheat the oven to 350°F (180°C). Butter a 9- × 13-inch (23 × 33 cm) baking pan or line the bottom and sides with parchment paper.

Cream together the butter and sugar in the bowl of a stand mixer fitted with the paddle attachment. Mix the flour and salt together in a small bowl. Slowly add the flour and salt and blend until the mixture is thoroughly combined.

Press the dough into the prepared pan, spreading evenly. Bake for 15 minutes.

Spread the jam evenly over the hot crust.

TOPPING

Mix the flour, rolled oats, brown sugar, and salt together in a large bowl.

Cream the butter in the bowl of a stand mixer fitted with the paddle attachment. Slowly add the dry ingredients and blend until the mixture is thoroughly combined.

Sprinkle the topping over the jam, spreading evenly. (Do not press the crumble down.) Bake the squares for an additional 25 minutes.

Cool to room temperature before slicing into approximately 2-inch (5 cm) squares.

STORAGE Store the squares in an airtight container for up to 5 days.

chocolate chip cookies

We think this is the ultimate chocolate chip cookie. We experimented with dozens of recipes and incorporated the advice of numerous "experts" until we came up with the cookie of everyone's dreams. Makes 12 large cookies.

½ cup (125 mL) unsalted butter, softened

½ cup (125 mL) firmly packed dark brown sugar

¼ cup (60 mL) granulated sugar

1 large egg

1 tsp (5 mL) pure vanilla extract

1⅔ cups (410 mL) all-purpose flour

¾ tsp (4 mL) baking soda

¾ tsp (4 mL) fine sea salt

¾ cup (185 mL) bittersweet chocolate chips

½ cup (125 mL) chopped toasted walnuts (see note on page 222)

Cream together the butter and sugars in the bowl of a stand mixer fitted with the paddle attachment. Add the egg and vanilla and mix for 1 minute on medium speed.

Sift together the flour, baking soda, and salt in a medium-sized bowl. Slowly add the dry ingredients to the wet ingredients until combined and the dough comes together in a ball. Add the chocolate and walnuts and mix until just combined.

Cover the dough tightly with plastic wrap and refrigerate for at least 30 minutes and up to 72 hours. (The longer the dough is allowed to chill, the more the flavours will be able to combine and develop.)

Preheat the oven to 350°F (180°C). Line a baking sheet with parchment paper.

For each cookie, take ¼ cup (60 mL) dough and form it into a ball. Place each ball on the baking sheet and press it into a 3-inch (8 cm) round, about ½ inch (1 cm) thick.

Bake for 10 minutes or until the cookies are golden brown, but still soft in the middle.

Transfer the cookies to a baking rack to cool.

STORAGE Store the cookies in an airtight container for up to 5 days.

▶ It may seem odd to add salt to baked goods, like these cookies, but it's an essential ingredient. It enhances and brightens the flavours of the other ingredients.

peanut butter cookies

Mila Klomp won 1st prize in the 9- to 12-year-old category for her yummy peanut butter cookies. It's clear that Mila has inherited her baking talent from her mom, Helen. (See page 161.) Makes 5 dozen.

1 cup (250 mL) granulated sugar
1 cup (250 mL) firmly packed
    brown sugar
1 cup (250 mL) shortening (or
    unsalted butter, softened)
1 cup (250 mL) peanut butter
2 large eggs, beaten
1 tsp (5 mL) pure vanilla extract
3 cups (750 mL) all-purpose flour
½ tsp (2 mL) fine sea salt
2 tsp (10 mL) baking soda
1 Tbsp (15 mL) hot water

THE
HARROW
FAIR

1st

Preheat the oven to 375°F (190°C). Line a large baking sheet with parchment paper.

Cream the sugars and shortening together in the bowl of a stand mixer using the paddle attachment. Add the peanut butter, eggs, and vanilla. Beat the dough at medium speed until thoroughly combined. Mix the flour and salt together in a small bowl. Slowly add the flour and salt to the dough and blend until the mixture is thoroughly combined. Combine the baking soda and hot water in a small bowl. Add to the dough, mixing until just combined.

Drop the dough by heaping tablespoons onto the baking sheet. Gently press a floured fork into each cookie, first vertically, then horizontally, creating the signature peanut-butter-cookie criss-cross.

Bake for 8 minutes or until the edges of the cookies begin to turn golden brown.

Transfer the cookies to a rack to cool.

STORAGE Store the cookies in an airtight container for up to 5 days.

▶ Mila is a member of the local 4-H Baking Club. Many members enter their favourite sweets in the Harrow Fair baking competitions.

4-H is an international organization that focuses on developing youth to their fullest potential. Traditionally focused on raising livestock, making handcrafts, and baking, today 4-H has many different clubs to suit all interests.

"Learn by doing" is the 4-H slogan.

sugar cookies

Baking sugar cookies is so much fun, especially with kids. Makes about 24 large cookies.

¾ cup (185 mL) granulated sugar
¾ cup (185 mL) unsalted butter,
  softened
1 large egg
1 tsp (5 mL) pure vanilla extract
2¼ cups (560 mL) all-purpose flour
¼ tsp (1 mL) fine sea salt
1 tsp (5 mL) cold water (approx)

In the bowl of a stand mixer fitted with the paddle attachment, cream together the sugar and butter until light and fluffy. Add the egg and vanilla and mix until blended.

Sift together the flour and salt in a small bowl. Gradually add the dry ingredients to the wet ingredients, mixing until they just come together. Add water, a few drops at a time, until the dough just starts to come away from the sides of the bowl.

Shape the dough into a flat disc and wrap in plastic wrap. Refrigerate for at least 2 hours. Allow the dough to warm and soften at room temperature for 15 minutes before rolling.

Preheat the oven to 350°F (180°C). Line a large baking sheet with parchment paper.

Roll out the dough to ⅛-inch (3 mm) thickness on a lightly floured surface. Cut the dough into shapes using your favourite cookie cutters. Re-roll the scraps until all the dough has been cut into cookies.

Bake for 8 minutes or until the edges of the cookies begin to turn golden brown.

Transfer to a rack to cool before frosting with royal icing.

STORAGE Store the cookies in an airtight container for up to 1 week.

royal icing

2 egg whites (see note)
1 cup (250 mL) sifted icing sugar
Fresh lemon juice, if needed
Natural food colouring

Beat the egg whites until foamy at high speed in a stand mixer fitted with the whisk attachment. Gradually add the icing sugar, about ½ cup (125 mL) at a time, waiting until it has been completely incorporated before adding more.

Continue beating at high speed until the icing is thick and shiny, about 10 minutes. The icing must be thick but not stiff. (It will remind you of glue.) If the icing is too thick, add a few drops of lemon juice until the correct thickness is reached.

Divide the icing into small cups and colour as desired.

▶ If there is concern about using raw egg whites for the icing recipe, cartons of pasteurized egg whites are available. Pasteurized egg whites have been heated to kill any harmful bacteria.

▶ Great tools for spreading royal icing on sugar cookies include pastry bags and tips, plastic squeeze bottles, knives, Popsicle sticks, and toothpicks.

gingersnaps

Cathy Reese's 1st prize–winning gingersnaps are everything they should be: crispy and chewy, sweet and spicy. Makes 5 dozen.

2 cups (500 mL) all-purpose flour
2 tsp (10 mL) baking soda
1 tsp (5 mL) ground cinnamon
1 tsp (5 mL) ground ginger
½ tsp (2 mL) ground cloves
¼ tsp (1 mL) fine sea salt
1 cup (250 mL) firmly packed
    brown sugar
¾ cup (185 mL) vegetable oil
¼ cup (60 mL) molasses
1 large egg
½ cup (125 mL) granulated sugar

Preheat the oven to 375°F (190°C). Line a large baking sheet with parchment paper.

Sift together the flour, baking soda, cinnamon, ginger, cloves, and salt in a large bowl.

Beat together the brown sugar, oil, molasses, and egg until combined in the bowl of a stand mixer using the paddle attachment. Slowly add the dry ingredients to the wet ingredients, mixing until fully combined.

Roll the dough into balls, about 1 heaping teaspoon (>5 mL) each. Place the granulated sugar in a small bowl. Roll the balls in the sugar.

Place the balls on the prepared sheet, but do not press down. Bake for 10 minutes.

Transfer the cookies to a rack to cool.

STORAGE   Store the cookies in an airtight container for up to 5 days.

▶ When baking cookies in batches, allow the hot baking sheet to cool before filling it with the next batch of cookie dough. It is handy to have at least two baking sheets going at the same time when you are working with large batches of cookie dough.

THE
HARROW
FAIR

1st

jam thumbprint cookies

When Moira's daughter, Ellen, was four years old, Ellen entered these cookies in the Harrow Fair. Not only did Ellen help make them, she also picked some of the raspberries that were used to make the jam. Her 1st prize ribbon was well deserved! Makes 18 cookies.

½ cup (125 mL) unsalted butter
¼ cup (60 mL) firmly packed brown
     sugar
1 large egg, separated
1 tsp (5 mL) pure vanilla extract
1 cup (250 mL) all-purpose flour
¼ tsp (1 mL) + 1 pinch fine sea salt
1 cup (250 mL) finely chopped toasted
     walnuts (see note on page 222)
½ cup (125 mL) raspberry jam (see
     note on page 6)

Preheat the oven to 350°F (180°C). Line a large baking sheet with parchment paper.

Beat the butter until it is light and fluffy in the bowl of a stand mixer fitted with the paddle attachment. Beat in the brown sugar. Add the egg yolk and vanilla, mixing until combined.

Sift together the flour and salt. Gradually add the dry ingredients to the wet ingredients, mixing until just combined.

Whisk together the egg white and a pinch of salt in a small bowl until it turns foamy. Place the chopped walnuts in a second small bowl.

Roll the dough into 1 Tbsp (15 mL) balls. Roll the balls in the egg white and then the chopped walnuts.

Place the cookies on the prepared baking sheet. Using your thumb, make a deep print in the middle of each cookie.

Bake for 5 minutes. Remove the cookies from the oven and press down the indentation again. (Use a wooden spoon this time—unless you have really tough thumbs!)

Bake for an additional 15 minutes. Transfer the cookies to a rack to cool.

While the cookies are cooling, place the raspberry jam in a small saucepan set over low heat. Cook for 3 minutes or until the jam has softened. Cool the jam for 5 minutes before spooning into the cookies. Fill each thumbprint with jam.

Cool completely before enjoying.

STORAGE Store the cookies in an airtight container for up to 5 days.

shortbread cookies

Elizabeth Ryan is a long-time resident of Harrow whose family was originally from Scotland. Not surprisingly, Elizabeth's recipe for shortbread is smooth and melt-in-the-mouth amazing. Her husband, Ty, was Harrow's milkman for decades, before becoming Harrow's mayor. Makes 100 cookies.

2 cups (500 mL) unsalted butter,
    softened
1 cup (250 mL) rice flour
1 cup (250 mL) berry sugar
3 cups (750 mL) all-purpose flour

Preheat the oven to 300°F (150°C). Line a 10- × 15-inch (25 × 38 cm) rimmed baking sheet with parchment paper.

Cream the butter in the bowl of a stand mixer fitted with the paddle attachment. In a medium-sized bowl, combine the rice flour, berry sugar, and flour. Slowly add the dry ingredients to the butter. Mix the dough on medium speed until it begins to come together in a ball.

Press the dough into the prepared baking sheet. Use a large rolling pin to distribute the dough evenly, making certain the corners are filled.

Using a table fork, prick up and down the entire surface of the dough, no more than ¼ inch (6 mm) apart.

Bake for about 45 minutes or until the cookies begin to turn a pale golden colour. Cool for 5 minutes, then cut into 1- × 1.5-inch (2.5 × 4 cm) rectangles. (Do not wait until the shortbread has cooled completely before cutting or it will be too difficult to cut.)

When the shortbread has completely cooled, remove the cookies from the pan.

STORAGE Store the shortbread in an airtight container for up to 1 week.

▶ Most traditional shortbread recipes contain some rice flour. It helps keep gluten development to a minimum, so the shortbread remains tender.

funnel cakes

Funnel cakes are found at country fairs across North America. They're made from a simple batter that is poured through a funnel into hot oil, in random circular patterns. Once they turn golden brown, they're sprinkled with icing sugar and served hot. Makes 12 large funnel cakes.

2 large eggs
1¾ cups (435 mL) milk
2 cups (500 mL) all-purpose flour
1 tsp (5 mL) baking powder
½ tsp (2 mL) fine sea salt
Vegetable oil, for frying
1 cup (250 mL) icing sugar

Combine the eggs, milk, flour, baking powder, and salt in a food processor. Mix until smooth, scraping down the sides as needed. Set aside.

Pour 3 inches (8 cm) of oil into a medium-large saucepan and heat to 375°F (190°C).

Pour ¼ cup (60 mL) of batter into the funnel, covering the bottom hole with your finger. Hold the funnel over the hot oil, carefully removing your finger, and move the funnel in circles in a sort of free-form lattice pattern. (It may take a few attempts to master this method.)

When the funnel cake becomes noticeably golden, turn it over and continue frying the other side.

Carefully remove the cake from the oil with a slotted spoon. Drain the cake on a plate lined with paper towels.

Before adding more batter to the oil, make sure the oil has returned to 375°F (190°C). Continue cooking the funnel cakes until all the batter is used.

Using a sieve, sprinkle the completed funnel cakes generously with icing sugar.

Enjoy immediately.

jam doughnuts

During the photo shoot for this cookbook, the chubbiest squirrel we've ever seen wad-dled over to our picnic table. He helped himself to a jam doughnut (which was sitting on the bottom of our carefully constructed pyramid) and took off up the nearest tree. He sat there for ages, staring at us and enjoying his doughnut. He may have been a thief, but he was our kind of thief. Makes 12 doughnuts.

2¼ tsp (11 mL) active dry yeast

1 tsp + ¼ cup (5 mL + 60 mL) granulated sugar, divided

½ cup (125 mL) water, heated to 110°F (43°C)

½ cup (125 mL) milk

¼ cup (60 mL) unsalted butter

1 tsp (5 mL) fine sea salt

2 cups (500 mL) all-purpose flour

1 large egg

½ cup (125 mL) homemade fruit jam (pages 3–7)

Vegetable oil, for frying

1 cup (250 mL) icing sugar

Soak the yeast and the 1 tsp (5 mL) sugar in the warm water for 10 minutes in the bowl of a stand mixer fitted with the paddle attachment.

Heat the milk in a small saucepan until bubbles form around the edges. Remove from the heat. Add the butter, the ¼ cup (60 mL) sugar, and salt, stirring until the butter melts. Cool the mixture until it is lukewarm. Add the milk mixture to the risen yeast. Add the flour and the egg.

Mix the dough for 5 minutes on medium speed.

Scrape the dough into a mound. Cover the bowl with plastic wrap, and let rise 2 hours in a warm, draft-free spot.

Punch the dough down, attach the dough hook to the stand mixer, and knead for 5 minutes at medium speed. Roll the dough out to a ¼-inch (6 mm) thickness. Let the dough rest in the refrigerator for 15 minutes. (The dough is very soft; this step makes the dough easier to handle.) Cut out circles with a 2½-inch (6 cm) round cutter and let stand another 5 minutes.

Place 1 heaping tsp (7 mL) of jam in the centre of half of the rounds. With a wet finger, moisten the edges around the jam. Top with the remaining rounds and seal the edges firmly. Let the doughnuts rise, uncovered, for 30 minutes.

Pour 3 inches (8 cm) of oil into a medium-large saucepan and heat to 350°F (180°C).

Carefully place no more than 2 or 3 doughnuts into the oil at one time. As they rise to the top of the oil and turn dark golden brown, turn them over. Each side will take about 3 minutes. Remove the doughnuts from the oil and drain on a plate lined with paper towel. Before adding more doughnuts to the oil, make sure the oil has returned to 350°F (180°C). Continue cooking in batches.

Continued . . .

jam doughnuts *(continued)*

After the doughnuts have been fried, let them cool for 10 minutes.

Using a fine sieve, dust both sides of the doughnuts with icing sugar before enjoying.

▶ While this recipe has been squirrel tested and approved, it's intended for people.

▶ We like using bumbleberry jam (page 6) in this recipe, but any jam will work well in these doughnuts as long as it is quite thick.

apple fritter rings

Slices of crisp, tart apples are dipped in batter, deep fried, and rolled in cinnamon sugar. These aren't made at the Harrow Fair, but if they were, it would be a very busy concession stand. Makes 3 dozen.

1 cup (250 mL) all-purpose flour
2 Tbsp (30 mL) cornstarch
1 Tbsp + ½ cup (15 mL + 125 mL)
   granulated sugar, divided
½ tsp (2 mL) baking powder
½ tsp (2 mL) fine sea salt
1 large egg
1 cup (250 mL) milk
½ tsp (2 mL) ground cinnamon
5 apples
Vegetable oil, for frying

Mix together the flour, cornstarch, the 1 Tbsp (15 mL) granulated sugar, baking powder, and salt in a large bowl.

Beat the egg and milk together in a medium-sized bowl. Whisk the wet ingredients into the dry ingredients, mixing well. Refrigerate the batter for 1 hour.

Mix the ½ cup (125 mL) granulated sugar with the cinnamon in a shallow bowl.

Peel and core the apples. Slice crosswise into rings, about ¼-inch (6 mm) thick.

Pour 1 inch (2.5 cm) oil into a medium-large saucepan and heat to 375°F (190°C).

Dip the apple rings in the batter, allowing the excess to drip back into the bowl. Fry 2 or 3 rings at a time, for 3 minutes or until golden brown, turning frequently. Drain the rings on a plate lined with paper towels.

Dredge the fritters in the cinnamon-sugar mixture.

Before adding more fritters to the oil, make sure the oil has returned to 375°F (190°C). Continue cooking until all the rings are fried.

Serve warm.

▶ For this recipe, the best apple varieties to use are those that tend to be tart, so their flavour isn't lost when paired with the other ingredients. Local varieties of suitable apples include Braeburn, Cortland, Granny Smith, and Honeycrisp.

frozen custard

Frozen custard is made with egg yolks, sugar, and cream, making this ice cream incredibly soft and rich. Makes 4 cups (1 L).

6 egg yolks
¾ cup (185 mL) granulated sugar
¼ tsp (1 mL) fine sea salt
2 cups (500 mL) whipping cream
2 cups (500 mL) milk
1 tsp (5 mL) pure vanilla extract

Prepare an ice cream maker according to the manufacturer's directions.

Whisk together the egg yolks, sugar, and salt in a medium-sized bowl until combined.

Heat the cream and milk in a saucepan set over medium heat, stirring occasionally. Add a small amount of the hot milk to the beaten egg mixture. Whisk the egg mixture into the saucepan with the rest of the milk. Cook on low heat, stirring constantly, for 5 minutes or until the custard coats the back of a spoon.

Strain the custard through a fine sieve, add the vanilla, and chill thoroughly.

Pour the mixture into the ice cream maker. Follow the manufacturer's instructions.

STORAGE   Freeze in an airtight container for up to 1 week.

▶ Invented in 1866 by a Detroit pharmacist, Vernors is one of America's oldest soft drinks. Being made just across the river in Detroit, Vernors is a local favourite. "Deliciously different," it is aged in oak barrels for 3 years and contains 19 ingredients including ginger and vanilla. For a classic float, try 2 scoops of frozen custard with Vernors.

melon creamsicles

These creamsicles are so delicious that it's downright shocking how easy they are to make. The trick is using very ripe, juicy cantaloupes or honeydew melons. Makes 6 creamsicles.

2 cups (500 mL) cubed fresh
    cantaloupe or honeydew melon
½ cup (125 mL) whipping cream
2 Tbsp (30 mL) honey
6 Popsicle sticks

Place the melon in a food processor. Process for 1 minute, until very smooth. Add the cream and honey. Process until well blended.

Pour the mixture into Popsicle moulds. Insert Popsicle sticks into the moulds. Freeze until solid.

Enjoy on a hot afternoon.

grape snow

This might be the easiest recipe in the whole book. Everyone loves this simple summertime treat. Makes 4 snowdrifts.

¼ cup (60 mL) berry sugar
¼ cup (60 mL) water
1¾ cups (435 mL) fresh Coronation
    grape juice (see note on page 212),
    or any good-quality grape juice

Place 4 small serving bowls in the freezer.

Place the sugar, water, and grape juice in an 8-inch (20 cm) square glass baking dish. Stir until the sugar is dissolved.

Freeze for 30 minutes. Using 2 forks, scrape any frozen crystals into the centre of the dish. Continue to freeze, scraping every 30 minutes, until the mixture is completely frozen and granular, about 4 hours total.

Pile the grape snow into 4 chilled bowls and serve.

grape ice cream

Outstanding. Seriously outstanding. This ice cream is so good, it's reason enough to invest in an ice cream maker. Makes 4 cups (1 L).

1¼ cups (310 mL) fresh Coronation grape juice (see note), or any good-quality grape juice
2 cups (500 mL) whipping cream
⅓ cup (80 mL) granulated sugar
1 Tbsp (15 mL) fresh lemon juice

Prepare an ice cream maker according to the manufacturer's directions.

Mix all the ingredients together in a large bowl until the sugar is dissolved.

Pour the mixture into the ice cream maker. Follow the manufacturer's instructions.

STORAGE Store the ice cream in an airtight container in the freezer for up to 1 week.

▶ CORONATION GRAPE JUICE To make your own grape juice, place 4 cups (1 L) Coronation grapes in a large saucepan. Simmer for 5 minutes over medium heat. Use a potato masher to crush the grapes, releasing the juice and the colour from the skins. Strain the grapes through a very fine sieve, reserving the juice. Discard the skins and pulp. Chill the juice thoroughly before proceeding with these recipes. The juice may also be frozen.

▶ The Coronation grape, a seedless varietal, was developed in Canada and has surpassed the much-loved Concord grape in popularity. The grape is a vibrant purple colour and it's very aromatic, with that classic grapey smell everyone can identify.

Coronation grapes are available in Essex County for a short time in late summer and early fall. Buy as many bunches as you can find, making the juice and freezing it until needed.

mint chocolate ice cream

Mint chocolate is an ice cream flavour everyone has had before. But when it's made at home from high-quality, fresh ingredients, it's an entirely new experience. Our version is softly flavoured with fresh mint and enhanced by just the right amount of bittersweet chocolate. Makes 4 cups (1 L).

¾ cup (185 mL) loosely packed fresh mint leaves
¾ cup (185 mL) granulated sugar
6 egg yolks
¼ tsp (1 mL) fine sea salt
2 cups (500 mL) milk
2 cups (500 mL) whipping cream
½ cup (125 mL) finely chopped bittersweet chocolate (see note on page 191)

Prepare an ice cream maker according to the manufacturer's directions.

Process the mint and sugar together in a food processor until the mint is finely chopped.

Whisk together the egg yolks, salt, and the sugar-mint mixture in a medium-sized bowl until thoroughly combined.

Heat the milk and cream in a saucepan set over medium heat, stirring occasionally. Add a small amount of the hot milk to the beaten egg mixture. Whisk the egg mixture into the saucepan with the rest of the milk. Cook over low heat, stirring constantly, for 5 minutes or until the mixture is thick enough to coat the back of a spoon.

Strain the custard through a fine sieve and chill thoroughly.

Fold in the chocolate. Pour the mixture into the ice cream maker. Follow the manufacturer's instructions.

STORAGE Freeze in an airtight container for up to 1 week.

strawberry shortcake ice cream

The idea for this ice cream was inspired by the classic summer dessert and the retro Popsicle of the same name. Moira's husband, Alan, finds it irresistible. He's been caught enjoying it in the middle of the night . . . his happy face illuminated by the soft glow of the freezer light. Makes 6 cups (1.5 L).

CRUMBLE
½ cup (125 mL) all-purpose flour
¼ cup (60 mL) unsalted butter, softened
⅓ cup (80 mL) firmly packed brown sugar

ICE CREAM
6 egg yolks
¾ cup (185 mL) granulated sugar
¼ tsp (1 mL) fine sea salt
2 cups (500 mL) whipping cream
2 cups (500 mL) milk
1 tsp (5 mL) pure vanilla extract
1½ cups (375 mL) crushed fresh strawberries

THE
HARROW
FAIR
———
authors'
FAVE

CRUMBLE
Preheat the oven to 350°F (180°C). Line a baking sheet with parchment paper.

Mix the flour, butter, and brown sugar together in a small bowl. Spread the mixture out on the baking sheet.

Bake for 10 minutes.

Cool the crumble to room temperature.

ICE CREAM
Prepare an ice cream maker according to the manufacturer's directions.

Whisk together the egg yolks, sugar, and salt in a medium-sized bowl until combined.

Heat the cream and milk in a saucepan set over medium heat, stirring occasionally. Add a small amount of the hot milk to the beaten egg mixture. Whisk the egg mixture into the saucepan with the rest of the milk. Cook on low heat, stirring constantly, for 5 minutes or until the custard coats the back of a spoon.

Strain the custard through a fine sieve, add the vanilla, and chill thoroughly.

Mix together the cold custard, crushed strawberries, and crumble in a large bowl. Pour the mixture into the ice cream maker. Follow the manufacturer's instructions.

STORAGE   Freeze in an airtight container for up to 1 week.

▶ To soften rock-hard ice cream, place the ice cream in the refrigerator and let it sit for about 45 minutes before serving. The inside and outside of the ice cream will soften evenly, making perfectly scoopable ice cream every time.

ice cream sandwiches

Ice cream sandwiches sounds like a dessert that's just for little kids. But when home-made ice cream is sandwiched between prize-winning cookies, it becomes a treat that's good enough to serve to kids of any age. Makes 12 sandwiches.

4 cups (1 L) ice cream, softened
24 homemade cookies

Line a 9- × 13-inch (23 × 33 cm) baking pan with plastic wrap, leaving long ends to fold back over the top.

Spread the softened ice cream in the pan in an even layer. The ice cream should be no more than 1 inch (2.5 cm) thick. Fold the plastic wrap over the ice cream and freeze until firm.

Cut out rounds of ice cream, using a cookie cutter or knife, slightly smaller than the cookies. Sandwich the ice cream between 2 cookies.

Serve immediately.

STORAGE Wrap the sandwiches in plastic wrap and store in the freezer. Serve within 24 hours.

Moira and Lori's favourite recipe combinations

Peanut butter cookies (page 198) + grape ice cream (page 212) = PB&J'wiches

Sugar cookies (page 201) + Strawberry Shortcake Ice Cream (page 215) = Strawberry Short'wiches

Chocolate chip cookies (page 197) + mint chocolate ice cream (page 213) = Mint Chocolate Choc'wiches

▶ The Harrow Fair's Homecraft Directors make and sell close to 4,000 ice cream sandwiches every year at the fair. The proceeds go toward improving the buildings at the fairgrounds.

candy apples

This recipe is a classic. But we've removed the red food colouring from the traditional recipe so the naturally rosy-red glow of the apples can shine through. Makes 12 candy apples.

12 red-skinned apples
3 cups (750 mL) granulated sugar
½ cup (125 mL) light corn syrup
1 cup (250 mL) water
12 Popsicle sticks

Wash and dry the apples thoroughly. Ensure the apples are crisp and unblemished. Remove the stems, and insert a Popsicle stick into each stem spot until secure.

Place apples on a large baking sheet lined with parchment.

Add the sugar, corn syrup, and water to a large saucepan set over medium heat. Set a wooden spoon, a glass of water, a pastry brush, and a candy thermometer beside the stove.

Use the wooden spoon to stir the mixture until it boils. Attach the candy thermometer to the side of the saucepan. Dip the pastry brush in the glass of water and brush down the sides of the saucepan to prevent sugar crystals from forming.

Continue to cook the mixture, without stirring, over medium heat. When the mixture reaches 300°F (150°C), immediately remove the saucepan from the heat.

Working quickly and carefully, twirl each apple until well coated with the hot candy.

Transfer to the baking sheet to cool.

STORAGE Place on a decorative platter or individually wrap each apple in cellophane and tie with a ribbon.

The apples will keep for 3 days.

▶ Local red-skinned apples suitable for making candy apples include McIntosh, Ida Red, Cortland, Red Delicious, Empire, and Gala.

salted peanut brittle

Simple, brittle candy made with peanuts and corn syrup began appearing in cookbooks in the 19th century. Our modern version is salty and sweet, buttery and nutty. It's an irresistible treat. Makes 1½ lb (750 g).

1 Tbsp (15 mL) unsalted butter
1 Tbsp (15 mL) baking soda
1 tsp (5 mL) fine sea salt
1 cup (250 mL) granulated sugar
1 cup (250 mL) corn syrup
3 cups (750 mL) shelled, roasted, and
salted peanuts

Line a large baking sheet with parchment paper or generously butter.

Place 1 Tbsp (15 mL) butter in a small bowl. Combine the baking soda and salt in another small bowl. Set the bowls, a wooden spoon, a glass of water, a pastry brush, and a candy thermometer beside the stove.

Combine the sugar and corn syrup in a medium-sized saucepan. With the wooden spoon, stir the mixture until it boils. Attach the candy thermometer to the side of the saucepan. Dip the pastry brush in the glass of water and brush down the sides of the saucepan to prevent sugar crystals from forming.

Continue to cook the mixture, without stirring. When the mixture reaches 295°F (146°C), remove the pan from the heat. Carefully stir in the peanuts. Add the butter and then the baking soda and salt.

Pour the hot peanut brittle onto the baking sheet. Using a buttered spatula, spread the brittle out as thinly as possible.

Let the brittle cool for at least 1 hour before breaking into bite-sized pieces.

STORAGE   Store in an airtight container for up to 2 weeks.

sponge toffee

You may not have even realized that it's possible to make something like sponge toffee at home. It's not only possible, it tastes just like the candy you remember from childhood. Makes about 1 lb (500 g).

2 Tbsp (30 mL) baking soda
2½ cups (625 mL) granulated sugar
⅔ cup (160 mL) corn syrup
⅓ cup (80 mL) water
2 tsp (10 mL) pure vanilla extract

Line a large baking sheet with parchment paper or generously butter.

Sift the baking soda into a small bowl, ensuring no lumps remain. Set the baking soda, a whisk, a glass of water, a pastry brush, and a candy thermometer beside the stove.

Combine the sugar, corn syrup, water, and vanilla in a large stockpot. Use the wooden spoon to stir the mixture over medium heat until it boils. Attach the candy thermometer to the side of the stockpot. Dip the pastry brush in the glass of water and brush down the sides of the stockpot to prevent sugar crystals from forming. Continue to cook the mixture without stirring. When the temperature reaches 300°F (150°C), remove the pot from the heat. Immediately whisk the baking soda into the mixture. The mixture will start to expand and bubble up.

Pour the toffee onto the baking sheet. Spread the toffee evenly around the sheet with a wooden spoon, to a thickness of about 1½ inches (4 cm).

Cool the toffee completely before breaking it into pieces.

STORAGE Store in an airtight container for up to 1 week.

maple caramel corn with nuts

The only problem with this Maple Caramel Corn, inspired by a version made by our aunt Carolyn Mallard, is trying not to eat it all at once. Makes 12 cups (3 L).

POPCORN
3 Tbsp (45 mL) vegetable oil
½ cup (125 mL) yellow popcorn
   kernels

NUTS
1 cup (250 mL) whole pecans, toasted
   (see note)
1 cup (250 mL) whole almonds,
   toasted (see note)

MAPLE CARAMEL
1 cup (250 mL) unsalted butter
2 cups (500 mL) firmly packed light
   brown sugar
¼ cup (60 mL) pure maple syrup
¼ cup (60 mL) corn syrup
1 tsp (5 mL) fine sea salt
1 tsp (5 mL) pure vanilla extract
½ tsp (2 mL) baking soda

THE
HARROW
FAIR
———
authors'
FAVE

POPCORN
Add the oil to a large stockpot set over medium-high heat.

Add the kernels. Shake the pot to coat the kernels with hot oil. Set a lid on the pot, but leave a small gap to allow steam to escape. Once the kernels begin popping, gently shake the pot to keep the kernels moving.

When the popping has slowed down, transfer the popcorn to a very large bowl. Remove any unpopped kernels.

Add the toasted nuts to the popcorn.

MAPLE CARAMEL
Melt the butter in a large saucepan set over medium heat.

Add the sugar, maple syrup, corn syrup, and salt and increase the heat to medium-high. Bring the mixture to a boil, stirring constantly. Reduce the heat to medium and set a timer for 5 minutes. Do not stir.

Remove the pan from the heat after the 5 minutes are up. Stir in the vanilla and baking soda.

ASSEMBLY
Immediately pour the maple caramel over the popcorn and nuts. Carefully toss to coat the popcorn and nuts fully. Spread the mixture out on a baking sheet lined with parchment paper.

Cool to room temperature before breaking into pieces and serving.

STORAGE   Store in an airtight container for up to 1 week.

▶ Southwestern Ontario is the only region in Canada temperate enough to grow popping corn.

▶ TO TOAST NUTS   Preheat oven to 325°F (160°C). Spread the nuts in 1 layer on a baking sheet. Bake for 8 to 10 minutes, stirring once, until they are darker in colour and their nutty fragrance is released. Setting a timer will help make sure you don't burn the nuts.

MUMS
PEACHES
GLADIOLI
NECTARINES
APPLES
PEARS

THANK YOU, THANK YOU!

Alan Sanders, Jake Elstone, Matt Maloney, Brenda Anger, Leslie & Doug Balsillie, Kelly Beaulieu, Taryn Boyd, James Chatto, Janet Cobban & Kris Ives at the John R. Park Homestead, John & Gaby Crawley, Elaine Duffy, Carla Dutton, Eric Farrell, Elaine & Dermot Feore, Pat Fitzpatrick, Elaine Fox, Karen Fox, Jeff Goslin, Karen & Larry Goslin, Sophie Goslin, Marie Hall, Jen Heaton & Bruce Krzeczkowski, Gayle Hedges, Maggie Hildebrand at L'Escoffier Kitchen Emporium, Kathryn Humphries, Diane & Tom Ingersoll, Maureen Jack, Carol Jenner, Frances Jenner, Jessica Jenner, Jill Klemme & Family, Helen Klomp, Mila Klomp, Evie & Al Kozleski, Janette Lawton, Annie Lawton-Scurfield & Paul Scurfield, Nancy Leonard, Elaine Lepp, Judith Lethby, Seconda Lethby, Vicki Lucier, Jimmy Lypps, Carolyn & Tom Mallard, Kate Maloney Guertin, Marc Mantha, Petra Martlock, Carolyn Erichsen McAdam, Mike McColl, Robert McCullough, John McDonald, Mary Ann McDonald, Sharon & Chuck McDonald, Susan McGinn, Rose McLean, Kristin Merz, Tara Meyer & Heidi Umphrey, Dawn Nadon, Kristine Newman, Anna Olson, Roberta & Don Parry, Linda Pavao, Francy Pearman, Carrie Piper-Hedges, Tom Pistor, Cathy Reese, Lisa Renaud, Ray Ring, Hilda Ryan, Matt Ryan, Max Sanders, Dennis Sanson, Lisa Slater, Carmen Smith, Grandma Lela Smith, Tamara Stimpson, Ellen Strobel, Albert Testa, Shaila & Ryan Visser, Margaret Watsa, Edith Woodbridge.

BAKING

SHOWRING ►

NEWTU

FLOWERS ◄

LIVESTOCK ►

◄ VEGETABLES

PRIZE-WINNING RECIPES

THE HARROW FAIR

1st

AUTHORS' FAVES

THE HARROW FAIR

authors' FAVE

INDEX

ABOUT THE AUTHORS

MOIRA SANDERS

A fifth-generation native of Harrow, Ontario, Moira grew up attending the town's annual fair. After graduating from St. Clair College's culinary and marketing programs, Moira worked in well-known restaurants and gourmet food emporiums across Canada, including Meinhardt in Vancouver and Senses in Toronto. She also ran the kitchen of a chateau-turned-cooking school in the Limousin region of France.

Moira lives in Mount Albert, Ontario, with her husband, Alan, and their children, Gavin and Ellen. She spends her free time writing her recipe blog, www.moirasanders.com.

LORI ELSTONE

Inspired by the horticulture of her hometown, Moira's younger sister is a graduate of the culinary program of St. Clair College and holds a Bachelor of Science degree from Brock University. Lori has worked extensively in the food and wine industry, notably in the Niagara region—as the manager and cheesemonger of de Luca's Cheese Market & Deli, in the kitchen of On the Twenty Restaurant, and in the vineyard of Cave Spring Cellars. Lori is a food writer working for several regional publications. Lori lives in St. Catharines, Ontario, with her husband, Jake, and their children, Hugh and Erica.

BETH GOSLIN MALONEY

Beth was raised in Kingsville, Ontario (the town just east of Harrow). She is a graduate of the University of Western Ontario. Specializing in marketing, design, and copywriting, Beth has worked for a number of upscale brands including Zingerman's, Artisanal, Martha Stewart, and Dean & DeLuca. Additionally, she consulted to the government of Australia, helping some of the country's top food, wine, and lifestyle companies expand into the American market.

Beth lives in New York City with her husband, Matt, and their son, Patrick. She returns to the north shore of Lake Erie every summer to visit friends and family. (Beth is first cousin to Moira and Lori. Their mothers, Karen and Sharon, are identical twins.)

ABOUT THE PHOTOGRAPHER

MIKE MCCOLL

Mike McColl is a chef and food photographer based in Burlington, Ontario, whose work can be seen in several award-winning cookbooks. He's also a big fan of the Harrow Fair! Check out more of his work at www.photoswithsauce.ca.